W9-BMN-239

YOUNG ATHLETES, COUCH POTATOES, AND HELICOPTER PARENTS

YOUNG ATHLETES, COUCH POTATOES, AND HELICOPTER PARENTS

The Productivity of Play

Jessica Skolnikoff and Robert Engvall

ROWMAN & LITTLEFIELD
Lanham • Boulder • New York • Toronto • Plymouth, UK

Published by Rowman & Littlefield
4501 Forbes Boulevard, Suite 200, Lanham, Maryland 20706
www.rowman.com

10 Thornbury Road, Plymouth PL6 7PP, United Kingdom

British Library Cataloguing in Publication Information Available

Library of Congress Cataloging-in-Publication Data
Skolnikoff, Jessica.
Young athletes, couch potatoes, and helicopter parents : the productivity of play / Jessica Skolnikoff
and Robert Engvall.
pages cm
Includes bibliographical references and index.
ISBN 978-1-4422-2979-2 (cloth : alk. paper) -- ISBN 978-1-4422-2980-8 (electronic)
1. Sports for children--Social aspects--United States. 2. Sports for children--United States. 3.
Physical education for children--United States. 4. Play--Social aspects--United States. 5. Parent
and child--United States. I. Engvall, Robert P. II. Title.
GV709.2.S495 2014
796.083--dc23
2013038147

♾ ™ The paper used in this publication meets the minimum requirements of
American National Standard for Information Sciences Permanence of Paper
for Printed Library Materials, ANSI/NISO Z39.48-1992.

Printed in the United States of America

CONTENTS

ACKNOWLEDGMENTS

We wrote this book because we thought the stories within and the concepts we've discussed with each other were worth telling others and thus would be worthy of writing about. We, of course, didn't do this alone. We should acknowledge the many contributions made by others, including our express appreciation to the Roger Williams University Foundation to Promote Scholarship and Teaching, which provided us course releases allowing us the time necessary to devote to this project.

We are also grateful to the many friends and colleagues who have listened to a variety of our presentations over the years, most specifically at popular culture/American culture conferences, and who have provided invaluable feedback and encouragement. Much of their feedback and questions provided the foundations for particular chapters within this work. Also, Jessica presented some of her original youth and activities level research at the American Anthropological Association and Society for Applied Anthropology Conference.

Thanks to Christen Karniski of Scarecrow Press for believing that our ideas were worth putting on paper, and to Bridget Fitzpatrick for giving us much-needed editing comments and critiques of our writing, as well as pushing us to consider other ideas as well.

Lastly, and most importantly, this book could not have been written without the contributions of parents, coaches, recreation directors, teachers, administrators, and, most of all, the kids, through their time and willingness to talk to us about their sporting experiences. It is their voices along with ours that we hope come through in this work.

We will forever be indebted to our parents for their support in our own sports endeavors from young children to grown adults and to our immediate families for putting up with us while we wrote this thing! Thank you! We hope that our children have as much fun with sport as we do—even if they choose not to spend valuable time analyzing it so often.

INTRODUCTION

This book arose from our common interests in sports and popular culture. We have had numerous discussions over the years ranging from "academic" debates about the place of sports in our society to informal conversations about our own sports fandom and our own involvement directly and indirectly in sports, both organized and formally and unorganized and informally. How sports affect our day-to-day lives has tended to be, we suppose quite naturally, a day-to-day conversation. From these conversations have developed a series of topics that we believe will be of interest to the reader. Some of these topics have been the basis of presentations we've made and research we've done concerning sports and the relationship between sports and popular culture. Others have merely been fodder for "water cooler" conversations that we've deemed worthy of not only *our* further examination but also, we believe, for others to read, and to compare and contrast with their own life experiences.

This isn't intended as a critique of sports or the sporting culture, as those critiques have been done and, in many cases, done well. "The overwhelming number of scholarly works within the field of sport criticism have long held sport socially, politically, and culturally suspect, a uniformity that remains apparent today" (Rosen 2007, 2). Rosen, himself, is a good source for an analysis of the history or evolution of American attitudes toward competition as seen through the lens of sports. Criticizing much of the excesses that surround sports in our society is relatively easy, as the targets seem to consistently grow larger.

It has often been said that "life gets in the way" when one makes plans for the future. Writing a book truly exemplifies the truth of that adage. In the throes of writing this book, the "marathon bombing" occurred in Boston, a city not too far from the campus where we both teach, and where one of us grew up in the suburbs. Both of us had friends in that very race that day, and the horrible juxtaposition of the joy of competition and dedication faced with the horror of terrorism, murder, and mayhem puts sports into context for all of us. The marathon bombing occurred on a Monday, and given the events of that nightmarish week for the city of Boston, numerous sporting events were cancelled or postponed, including games featuring the Celtics, Bruins, and Red Sox. By Saturday, the Red Sox welcomed the fans back to Fenway Park with a celebration of the Boston police and others who worked so hard to respond to the events of the Monday before. Whether or not sports assisted in the "healing" of the city, is open, we suppose, to interpretation. But we are not the first to suggest that, at a minimum, sports contributed to a return to "normalcy." The premise that sports contribute to the quality of our lives, both directly and indirectly, seems almost self-evident. The return to the playing fields in both Major League Baseball and the National Football League several days after September 11, 2001, also served to return a sense of the routine and the comfortable to an unsteady and shaken country. When the Yankees returned to play after 9/11, there were many signs throughout baseball stadiums expressing sentiments like "we are all New Yorkers now," suggesting that the collective camaraderie of sports fans does have the potential to bring people together even across deeply partisan rooting lines.

The marathon bombing, like the events of September 11, showed both the relative unimportance of sports in the context of life, and the difference sports make and thereby the "importance" of sports in our lives. Just as wonderful and traditional celebrations of the sporting life can go horribly awry given the actions of a dangerous few, so too can we recognize the contributions that sports makes in the quality of our individual and collective lives. One didn't have to like baseball to recognize the cathartic nature of what happened at Fenway Park on that Saturday for the city of Boston. A gathering of thirty-five thousand or so people cheering in unison for the city, its first responders, and police force wasn't *because* of a baseball game, but it was made possible and practical *by* a baseball game. Similarly, perhaps, numerous July Fourth fireworks celebrations center around baseball games, and many of the families in attendance at both major and minor league ballparks gather more for the fireworks after the game than the game. Baseball becomes a family event, even for those uninterested in the game itself.

It wasn't our intention to begin this book with a nod to the intersections between sports and tragic events. In fact, Gavin (2012) has already addressed this more fully as the subject of his book *Sports in the Aftermath of Tragedy: From Kennedy to Katrina*. Still, as we write about sports in different contexts, life gets in the way, and thus our initial nod to the events happening all around us, which seem to almost force us to at least acknowledge their importance upon our culture, before we proceed. Then, just when we thought it safe to stick our toes back into the sporting water and find the goodness that sports and athletic competition can provide, the summer of 2013 in New England found us following the tale of an NFL player now implicated in a murder. Perhaps each individual story provides the backdrop for the larger story of how sports, competition, and even mere physical activity truly affect our day-to-day lives. It would seem probable that, like many books about sports and youth sports particularly, picking apart long-held notions of the goodness of the enterprise through a variety of anecdotal horror stories would lead inescapably to the conclusion that youth sports is in danger of assisting us in a more complete and more rapid descent into hell (or at least somewhere in a handbasket). Rosen (2007) suggested as much in his summary of sporting literature:

> The growing tendency to view competition, especially in its most recognizable form as competitive sport and its associative elements, as anathema to progress as well as antithetical to the values of a progressive people . . . indicate[s] that sport in the modern context can no longer measure up as either a beneficial or even a serviceable feature of American culture. (7)

It would appear that our work is cut out for us. A book that acknowledges the issues associated with youth sports in our culture cannot gloss over the many warts that are present and noticeable to all of our eyes. The hard part may lie in writing that book with a balanced approach that acknowledges the many flaws without abandoning the intended principles and joys that sports bring. Many of us, for example, play golf or tennis or run as both a means of staying in shape and because these pursuits bring us joy. The fact that many of us show little to no improvement in our abilities, despite years of "practice" might suggest that our time should be spent on something more valuable. Still, we run, we golf, we hit tennis balls all too often into the net, not because we think we will actually be good at these pursuits or because our practice time will make us better, but frankly, we do these things because we enjoy these things. Like the simple pleasure of reading a good novel, we do these things because we like to do these things; we do these things because they improve the enjoyment of our lives. Very rarely do people who enjoy a good novel become acclaimed novelists themselves. Similarly, merely playing golf or tennis does not often result in acclaim. But these pleasures do result in greater life satisfaction, and our rhetoric suggests that what we want most for our children is simply for them to be happy and contented. Despite the pressures we often put upon our children to excel in various sporting events, or the pressure we put upon ourselves to make every opportunity available to our children, the simple truth remains that we do these things because we want to do these things; it is important to recognize the same for our children and only "require" them to engage in activities if they truly enjoy those activities.

Despite the academic reality that finds us teaching in different disciplines, we have tried to write a book that combines our shared research, informed beliefs, and frankly, in some cases, simply our opinions as formed by our individual and shared experiences. We have tried to write this book in a way in which it is free of the constraints of either or both of our disciplines and of our long-shaped disciplinary perspectives. Free of those constraints, we attempt to examine sports from the perspectives of college professors who are fans, and who must temper our respective "fanaticisms" in order to observe in as neutral a manner as we can a variety of subjects that touch the "sporting life."

Our specific topics have included the nature of "helicopter parenting" and the impact that hyperinvolved parents have upon the "play" of their children. From this beginning, the book you hold in your hands features chapters that address a variety of topics under a broader theme that suggests that the nature of "play" has changed in our society, and while the reasons vary, most center upon greater involvement of parents into their children's lives, for good and for ill. Discussions about the pressures that are placed upon parents of athletic children, as well as the children themselves, will provide contrast to still other discussions concerning the pressures placed upon parents of children who do not achieve success in athletics, and thus must face a set of different pressures with potentially stigmatizing effects. While we live in a culture where accomplishment and success is congratulated and emphasized to a degree far exceeding any sort of egalitarian ethos, we thus live in a society where the pressure to succeed can often be overwhelming. That's not newsworthy. What we hope is different about this work is the way in which we address issues of athleticism that correspond to the greater divides in our society.

One chapter focuses on how children are chosen for their various sports teams. Another chapter concerns how the lack of unstructured play has lessened children's ability to resolve disputes and pursue their own interests, rather than interests their parents choose for them. Still another seizes upon the notion of "specialized sports" at a young age, so that in our hypercompetitive society parents can be comforted by the notion that their kids are "getting a jump" on other kids or at least staying even with other kids who are already specializing at a young age. These topics all lend themselves to individual chapters held together by the common theme that suggests that children's lives have increasingly become micromanaged by their parents.

That there is tremendous pressure upon parents, children, coaches, and all involved is hardly deniable any longer. Whether or not that pressure is justified is another topic entirely. Books have been written ranging from Callahan's *The Cheating Culture* (2004) to Best's *Everyone's a Winner* (2011), which when taken together seem to suggest a cultural phenomenon that requires success, even if it is somewhat artificial or unearned success. Cheating to gain an advantage, whether in the sporting world or the nonsporting world, has become central to the American thought process. Even for those who abhor the notion, it remains a central part of our lives as we watch the news and see political, social, and business leaders frequently embroiled in one scandal or another, most of which involve some level of an attempt to gain an unfair advantage over others. Whether or not we see cheating as part of the American way of life—"if you aren't cheating, you aren't trying"—or as symbolic of the decline of the human race, it remains a central feature of life as we know it. "Innocent" activities often involve some level of deception that makes us uncomfortable, even as we intellectually understand the implications of our actions. Take, for example, Ron and Kathie Smith's book *Slam for Life: The Story of a Girl's AAU Basketball Team* (2011), which features a story involving their own inner conflict with the concept of teaching their young daughter the necessary evil of telling a "white lie." The Smiths' convey their own story of their daughter's interest in playing organized basketball at a young age. Unfortunately, her interest came too early, as she was too young to be allowed to play on an organized team. They were faced with the unenviable choice of quashing her desire to play at that time or allowing her to join a team, which would require the "white lie" of fudging her age upward. They chose the latter and expressed their conflict over teaching their daughter honesty and integrity while also encouraging her to lie in this instance. As with many stories, perhaps the nature of a lie rests almost entirely with who tells it. Some people, no doubt, when faced with this decision would have no issue: she's not old enough, the rules are the rules, there really is no discussion, you either follow the rules as an honest person would do or break the rules as a dishonest person would do . . . what's to discuss? Putting it so simply seems terribly unfair to the parent just trying to do right by their child, but then again, what is the purpose of a rule if the rule is being circumvented? In their defense, of course, these parents simply wanted their daughter to play, quite different from more "typical cheating" in which one lies or engages in deceitful conduct in order to gain an advantage. Still, the reality of cheating even in this "harmless" way may mean that someone "more qualified" (in this case meaning of proper age) will not be allowed to play, as the roster would already be filled. Even the most minor "crimes" have victims, and when rules are broken, someone is necessarily harmed, even if that harm is not immediately apparent.

The way in which we rationalize our behavior transcends almost every activity in which we engage. We, and we suspect those of you reading this as well, have many times been stuck in traffic as we sit in the "proper" lane while we watch those passing us on the right, in the "exit" lane, cut in as they near the exit. Are we simply "dupes" who sit and wait while the "smart" people cut out from behind us and then cut in ahead of us? Or are we honest and filled with integrity so that we can feel better about ourselves as we walk into our scheduled appointments later than we otherwise would have? After experiencing traffic in this manner with some regularity, do we leave earlier for our appointments knowing that some people will "cheat" us and cost us valuable time? Or do we become part of the "cheating culture" ourselves and become somewhat more aggressive on the roadways?

If you lie to me, I am offended. If I lie to you, I had a valid reason. Getting one's young daughter onto a basketball team is not exactly breaking into Democratic headquarters, but still it points up the cultural acceptability many of us find in telling lies—so long as they are "harmless white lies." Perhaps you remember the story of Danny Almonte, the Little League pitcher who was virtually unhittable. It seemed as though he was a man among boys as the twelve-year-olds he faced simply couldn't touch his pitching. As it turned out, you probably remember, Danny really was in some sense a man among boys, as he (and his guardians) had consistently lied about his age so that his four-teen-year-old talents could be used to dominate his twelve-year-old opponents. As we discovered this deception, most of us were at some level outraged, saddened, and left lamenting the nature of our society in which it seemed important enough to someone to dominate Little League baseball, to do so through a series of lies and distortions meant to gain unfair advantage. Little League baseball, as American as apple pie, had officially gone the way of the soap box derby (another American pop cultural phenomenon famous for its "American-ness"), in which a serious cheating scandal threatened to forever tarnish the institution.

This book is not meant to criticize parents or other adults who are properly involved in children's lives, but is instead intended to address the structural and cultural changes that have fundamentally altered the way in which children play and the way in which children's sports are viewed in our society. All of us have heard the old adage concerning "all things in moderation," and ultimately that may be good advice for parents' level of involvement in their children's athletic activities. Over the years, the level of parents' involvement in their children's activities has evolved from possibly too little to probably too much. Many of us who are no longer young, when we reflect upon the level of involvement our parents had in our athletic lives, might recall that our parents seldom if ever attended our games. They surely never talked to our coaches or even seemed to ask us many questions about our sporting lives. Today, we have become all too familiar with the parents on the sidelines berating coaches, officials, and even the players, including their own children. Too much involvement, like too little, can be harmful. Achieving some level of moderation would seem to be the best advice money could buy.

Headlines in major newspapers have recently addressed exercise and its relationship to childhood obesity, the relationship between exercise and improved academic focus, and even the first lady's focus upon the importance of diet and exercise in improving the health of our children. The concepts of "helicopter parents" and "tiger moms" have also been addressed in the mainstream media, suggesting that interest in these topics is present and a book addressing specific concepts within the broader topic is ready for dissemination. The book you hold in your hands is that book.

We are mostly commenting on middle- to upper-class youth who are brought up in suburban areas. These "targets" of our commentaries are targets not because they are better or worse than other potential targets, but because they are the ones with which we are most familiar. Our emphasis in no way suggests that there will not always be room for ongoing discussions about race and class and how those variables affect youth participation, parental involvement, access to resources, and other salient issues. While acknowledging that reality, the focus of this work drew its conclusions largely from interviews and observations conducted with middle- to upper-class youth in mostly suburban areas. We do draw on some examples outside this group, particularly in the context of Amateur Athletic Union events, but not to the extent that we draw upon the former group.

We hope that this conversation is of potential interest to parents, coaches, athletic directors, and educators more generally, as a means of better understanding the culture that presently surrounds youth sports. Perhaps more grandly, we hope that it might even make a difference, if only to raise more questions and seek more appropriate answers regarding organized sports in our culture and the place sports (and play) should occupy in our and our children's lives.

The perceptions that people carry toward sports perhaps begin and end with their own anecdotal experiences and how those experiences have shaped their mostly positive or their mostly negative view toward sports generally. Our memories of sports frequently involve far more than whether we won more than we lost or whether our teams struggled on the field, although some of those memories can be lasting, particularly it seems the losses. Usually, our memories consist of the friends we made; the coaches, both good and bad; and the travel and other social aspects of the games. Those memories forge our lasting impressions, and become the dividing line between those who admire the virtues of sports and how sports might positively impact children and those who lament the vices of sports and view their impact as more negative than positive. There are many books that discuss youth and sports today and many that we have drawn upon to inform the conversations to follow in this book. To name a few: *Let the Kids Play: How to Stop Other Adults from Ruining Your Child's Fun and Success in Youth Sports* (Bigelow et al. 2001); *When Play Was Play: Why Pick-up Games Matter* (Bishop 2009); *Game On: The All-American Race to Make Champions of Our Children* (Farrey 2008); *101 Ways to Be a Terrific Sports Parent* (Fish and Magee 2003); *Whose Game Is It, Anyway? A Guide to Helping Your Child Get the Most from Sports, Organized by Age and Stage* (Ginsburg et al. 2006); *The Cheers and the Tears: A Healthy Alternative to the Dark Side of Youth Sports Today* (Murphy 1999); *The Overscheduled Child: Avoiding the Hyper-Parenting Trap* (Rosenfield and Wise 2001); and *Warrior Girls: Protecting Our Daughters against the Injury Epidemic in Women's Sports* (Sokolove 2008). Many of these titles have common themes including sections concerning parent behavior. Gone are the days when parents could only look to Dr. Spock's *Baby and Child Care* (1946) if they sought help in the literature in raising their children. Today we have thousands of books and a vast array of resources to assist us as we do our best to navigate the treacherous waters of parenthood. Not all of these resources, of course, feature entirely consistent advice or information, and thus our own "trial and error" and efforts to do our best to "muddle through" also shape the direction our own parenting takes.

In reviewing books for our research we found one specifically geared toward teens to help them navigate their sports experience. Gail Fay (2013) in her book *Sports: The Ultimate Teen Guide* sets out to help teens find their place in sports. She writes, "This book is written for anyone who loves to compete" (xii). Perhaps even more significantly, many of the topics she addresses are topics that much younger athletes need to consider. She does not address parent involvement and behaviors in their children's sporting experience. We have also considered many books written by journalists, sociologists, psychologists, anthropologists, parents, and coaches targeted toward parents and how they are involved in both positive and negative ways, but little has been written purposefully to help these young people work with their sports parents. As Joel Fish, author of *101 Ways to Be a Terrific Sports Parent* (2003), points out, "Yes, coaches, teammates, and the sport he plays matter. But the most critical factor in whether the forty million sports-playing children love their sports experience or hate them is the behavior—both public and private—and the attitude of their parents. This fact surprises many parents" (xiv). The fact that our children might be influenced by their parents' attitudes and behavior should be anything but surprising. Just as parents influence a child's development outside of sports, so too do they have tremendous influence over how a child perceives sports, and whether or not that child becomes an active participant in sports.

Our work attempts to navigate the fine line between our own admiration for "sporting culture" as fans and participants ourselves and our academic natures and professional realities, which have made us wary of many of the long-held "conventional wisdoms" surrounding the virtues of sports and athletics. How our sporting culture affects and pertains particularly to young people in our society is awash in contradictions. These contradictions range from the perceived virtues of learning teamwork and cooperation to the increased emphasis upon a "me-first" and hypercompetitive lifestyle that certainly allows for the sharing, anecdotally and otherwise, of as many negative experiences as positive ones. Even if we pay minimal attention to popular culture, as reported in the news media and the popular media, we are all very much aware of situations that have long taken the sheen off of professional sports. We have endured murder trials of NFL players (O. J. Simpson, Rae Carruth, Aaron Hernandez), sexual assault allegations involving boxing and the NBA (Mike Tyson, Kobe Bryant), and a myriad of "character" flaws that have followed professional sports and have merged into what Callahan (2004) referred to as the "cheating culture." From performance enhancing drugs in baseball and cycling to brain injury concerns in the National Football League (NFL) and National Hockey League (NHL), the luster that once belonged to professional sports has long worn away. Whether the "cheating culture" shapes the evolution of sports in our society or whether sports has been ahead of its time in advancing cheating to something of an art form, the romanticism that used to suggest sports as an entirely virtuous way of building character in the young and old alike has dissipated. Still, as if to point out the many contradictions of our sporting lives, our familiarity with the "cheating culture" has not diminished our individual beliefs in integrity in our own sporting lives. Those of us who play golf are all familiar with the variances among golfers of all abilities, as we all must resign ourselves to the vagaries of the game, and do not improve our lies or otherwise engage in the cheating culture because it simply isn't the right thing to do. Playing by the rules and doing the right things surely still exists in society at large, just as it does on the golf course. Yet, for all those who do play by the rules, it would seem that just as many do indeed "improve their lies"—a rather interesting play on words that pertains to golf, just as it does to the rest of our lives. There may simply be a fundamental difference between those who "improve their lies" and those who do not, and both sides of the spectrum can be found in every sporting venue just as they can be found in every venue outside of the sporting world. Many who engage in some "little white lies" on the golf course are quick to point out that they are not professionals, and golf is punishing enough without subjecting oneself to the humiliations sure to follow bad lies in the grass or behind bushes or trees. Thus, it is only practical to improve one's enjoyment of the game by "tweaking" the rules here and there. Perhaps for many, the sports culture follows that simple pattern of cheating "just a bit" in order to gain an advantage that will improve one's enjoyment of the game. It is difficult to separate the pervasive cheating culture from sports, just as it is difficult to separate that aspect of our lives from the rest of culture.

Decades ago when NBA superstar Charles Barkley famously denied that he was any type of role model (in response to his own transgressions involving alleged violence off the court), we perhaps should've listened more fully. "Sir Charles" has almost completely rehabilitated himself in the public eye and plays a significant role as a commentator on NBA coverage and as a commercial spokesperson. His notion that athletes should not be considered the role models for our children, and that instead that should be a burden placed upon parents and others who actually know and interact with individual children, was a good one. Perhaps it was always unfair to expect our athletes to be less flawed than the rest of us, but given their fame and relative fortunes, it would seem as though we have traditionally hoped for more than we've gotten in many cases.

It would seem like recognizing parents rather than famous people we do not know as our effective role models would be simple common sense, but doing so in reality is not always so easily implemented, and even when done, role modeling appropriately is often as difficult for parents as it is for famous athletes. The issues that parents often bring to youth sports, from violence on the sidelines, to verbal and even physical abuse of officials and coaches, to the unreasonable pressure exerted upon child athletes, suggest that many well-documented instances exist that would question parents' abilities to serve as proper sporting role models for their and other people's children. Perhaps the success of sports, like all other socially constructed events, as "worthy" examples for our children is wholly dependent upon the participants themselves. In essence, and again as common sense might suggest, good parenting provides for good childhood experiences, and less-skilled parenting provides for lesser-quality childhood experiences. The fact that children overcome a wide variety of less-than-stellar parental performances in their day-to-day lives should perhaps lessen the pressure placed upon our individual parenting moves, just as it might emphasize the importance of doing the best we can in our day-to-day lives. As Ginsburg, Durant, and Baltzell (2006) state in their book, *Whose Game Is It, Anyway?*:

> Finding a balance in challenging and supporting children in athletics requires diligence and sensitivity, and any approach must evolve over time as our kids grow up. As parents we have to do our homework and learn about our children, keep our own personal agendas in check, and discover what actually helps them have fun and thrive in sports. This is much easier said than done. (120)

Doing the best we can has long been the goal of many parents, and encouraging our children to model that behavior, by simply always doing the best they can, applies as well to life as it does to sports. The recognition that parents need to evolve just as their children develop and allow children to take the lead in how involved or how uninvolved they want to be in sports is difficult for many to accept. Just as some people simply expect their children to follow in the "family business," and have great difficulty allowing children to follow a different path, it is similarly difficult for parents who love sports and/or who were themselves very involved in sports to let children choose a different route.

The following chapters provide the reader with a variety of perspectives regarding youth sports. Some necessarily raise questions about the wisdom of the way in which we have raised our children in the sporting culture. Others suggest alternatives and express hope for a future in which some of the ills commonly associated with youth sports might be addressed.

Chapter 1 expands upon popular culture's interest in those who are perceived to be the most successful. We examine through the lens of youth sports the concept of those who achieve the "most" or those whom Gladwell (2008) describes as "outliers." The two authors of this chapter combine their "academic" backgrounds with their "real-world" experiences to create another take on the popular cultural phenomenon of youth sports. Ultimately we hope to establish that many of our best athletes no doubt are considered our best athletes because of their outstanding and "outlying" abilities that transcend the more common abilities that many possess. Yet, there is another powerful reason that many of these athletes have become elite; that reason lies at least in part in a rather "unnatural selection" process that separated them from their "less able" peers at relatively young ages.

Chapter 2 focuses upon the influence that "helicopter parents" have, not only upon their own children but also upon American culture. As college professors, we have become familiar with the term "helicopter parents"—a phrase that has been defined in popular culture as consisting of those parents who rush to prevent any harm or failure that might befall their children by hovering closely by and essentially attempting to control any and all outcomes. While that may be a rather generic definition of the term, and one that certainly applies to educators who receive phone calls from Mom or Dad about a son or daughter, it also applies more and more to those parents who hover around youth activities, and particularly for our purposes, Little League fields. Helicopter parents, in this context, attempt to influence and control the outcomes of children's games, and that may explain why we, as college professors who see these kids a decade later, still must often deal with parents who have honed their skills in manipulating others on Little League fields. If a parent on a Little League field, or a parent who watches his or her son or daughter perform in the orchestra or in a theatrical production, has had some success in influencing benefits that have accrued to the child, then why should we be surprised when these parents attempt, years later, to make certain that benefits accrue to their now college-aged child?

The irony, perhaps, lies not only on the children who are compelled to determine their life course while they believe in Santa Claus and the Tooth Fairy, but also upon the parents who believe Santa will actually deliver to them a major leaguer, or at least a collegiate scholarship. The idea that all children will simply be able to enjoy playing the game of baseball may now be in the past, given the pressures exerted upon them, having gone by the wayside just like the idea of being able to afford to take the family to Fenway Park. The ultimate goal of this chapter is to foster increased discussion of whether or not children's sports programs are in danger of having their worthwhile objectives of fostering character development, teamwork, discipline, and so forth, perverted into an environment in which what is actually learned is the importance of parental influence and incivility. We hope that by using Little League baseball as a lens through which we view parental influence and behavior that we contribute to the larger discussion of increased incivility in our society and the role of sports in American culture.

One of the many sports-related topics that long has interested us has been the concept of "athletic capital," which we define in chapter 3 as the high status that accrues to athletes in the United States generally and specifically to developing athletes in our middle schools. We argue here that the lack of athletic capital negatively impacts the physical activity level of those who do not possess it and that this has cultural as well as health consequences to those students. Data is drawn from observation, participant observation, and more than forty interviews with middle school children, parents, and educators in the midwestern, northeastern, and southern United States.

Sedentary lifestyles and obesity have become a national concern. Through participant observation and interviews with middle school–age youth, parents, physical educators, coaches, school administrators, school nurses, and youth organization directors, chapter 4 investigates youth dispositions toward physical activity across the United States. How children develop attitudes and habits related to exercise and physical activity is a multivariate issue. The holistic approach of anthropology can contribute to a multidisciplinary understanding of what should be a national concern. One area highlighted is the widening gap between children with athletic skills and access to play as compared to those with little ability and/or access. Youth sports have always been competitive but now as sports become the ticket to other opportunities the atmosphere is changing. Young children are pressured into "specializing" in one sport so they can become more proficient. No longer can Johnny or Jane try a sport at twelve for the sake of trying because their peers have been training since age five in order to be competitive. Coupled with the ever-growing pressure for public school systems to teach to the test, there is increasing pressure not to provide school time for physical activity and for learning games and sports; some schools are even dropping recess time. Where does this leave teaching and learning physical activity as a lifelong habit? Are we teaching our youth that only competitive athletes need physical activity? Or that participating in sports purely for enjoyment is a poor and unproductive use of one's time? This research starts to illuminate the relevance of social and cultural values that affect long-term beliefs and behaviors about physical activity.

Examining the power of play requires us to examine in chapter 5 the possibility that what is truly needed is a paradigm shift in schools that recognizes the interrelationship between academic achievement and physical education. Our rhetoric often suggests that we recognize the important interplay between physical health and academic success, but our practice and particularly our time devoted to physical education tends to betray that rhetoric. Schools must accept the responsibility for educating the whole person, and the power of play is an integral factor in creating confidence and the willingness to meet the challenges of an ever increasingly complex role as an adult. Many of our adult workplaces now encourage a certain level of physical activity, and with the constant rise in the price of health care, many companies even offer employees incentives to maintain a healthy lifestyle and thereby promote fewer health-care needs and costs.

Most young children, no matter what their athletic ability, start out enjoying gym class. To them it is an extension of play. That attitude frequently begins to change somewhere around the transition from fifth to sixth grade. If schools could or would take steps to stem the turning tide against the negative perceptions of gym class, or if they had a mandate to focus and support healthy activity, we could conceivably have healthier and more self-directed children and adults. We are all familiar with the term "lifelong learning" and generally that is a concept with an almost universal appeal. In contrast, we haven't always promoted "lifelong physical learning" in order to better achieve a healthier populace, despite its obvious benefits for our society, including the all-important and ever-emphasized economic benefits associated with better health.

Most of the debates in the United States about education are focused on assessment and teaching to the tests. While these debates continue, schools are cutting cocurricular activities such as physical education, music, and art. Physical education is too often considered merely as an add-on or is perceived as a babysitter or as only a place where students can blow off steam before they get back to their more-worthwhile pursuits. But given the current obesity epidemic that has serious implications for physical and mental development, a more active lifestyle plays a role in the development of a more-involved younger generation, and the role of physical education in our schools would seem to naturally assist us in that development.

There continue to be increasing demands on school administrators to replace time for physical activity with classroom instruction. Because of the priorities set by the federal government, district budget crises, union contract limits on working hours, lack of respect for physical education, risk management, and student choices between "cocurricular activities," there is little room left for physical education in the curriculum.

Why isn't being physically active more important in these contexts? As more and more parents are restricting their children from playing outside in their neighborhoods because of fear, wouldn't it be more sensible and effective to upgrade physical education in the curriculum? Instead of marginalizing physical education, might we consider that this could be the starting point for training healthier children who will become healthier adults?

Chapter 6 takes a look at the increasing influence of individualism upon our culture and how that affects youth sports. The idea that team comes first, and that individual performance should take a backseat to the noble concepts of teamwork, cooperation, and sacrifice for the greater good, is not always consistent with the way in which we are presently engaging our children and ourselves in the sporting culture.

Chapter 7 ends our discussion by using popular culture to inform a larger consideration of what has been lost in the ever-evolving world of youth sports.

WORKS CITED

Best, Joel. *Everyone's a Winner: Life in Our Congratulatory Culture*. Berkeley: University of California Press, 2011.

Bigelow, Bob, Tom Moroney, and Linda Hall. *Just Let the Kids Play: How to Stop Other Adults from Ruining Your Child's Fun and Success in Youth Sports*. Deerfield Beach: Health Communications, Inc., 2001.

Bishop, Ronald. *When Play Was Play: Why Pick-up Games Matter*. Albany: State University of New York Press, 2009.

Callahan, David, *The Cheating Culture: Why More Americans Are Doing Wrong to Get Ahead*. Orlando, FL: Harcourt, Inc., 2004.

Farrey, Tom. *Game On: The All-American Race to Make Champions of Our Children*. New York: ESPN Books, 2008.

Fay, Gail. *Sports: The Ultimate Teen Guide*. Lanham, MD: Scarecrow Press, 2013.

Fish, Joel, and Susan Magee. *101 Ways to Be a Terrific Sports Parent*. New York: Fireside Books, 2003.

Gavin, Michael. *Sports in the Aftermath of Tragedy: From Kennedy to Katrina*. Lanham, MD: Scarecrow Press, 2012.

Ginsburg, Richard, Steven Durant, and Amy Baltzell. *Whose Game Is It, Anyway? A Guide to Helping Your Child Get the Most from Sports, Organized by Age and Stage*. Boston: Houghton Mifflin Company, 2006.

Gladwell, Malcom. *Outliers: The Story of Success*. New York: Little, Brown, and Company, 2008.

Murphy, Shane. *The Cheers and the Tears: A Healthy Alternative to the Dark Side of Youth Sports Today*. San Francisco: Jossey-Bass Publishers 1999.

Rosen, Joel. *The Erosion of the American Sporting Ethos: Shifting Attitudes toward Competition*. Jefferson, NC: McFarland & Company, Inc., 2007.

Rosenfield, Alvin, and Nicole Wise. *The Overscheduled Child: Avoiding the Hyper-Parenting Trap*. New York: St. Martin's-Griffin, 2001.

Smith, Ron, and Kathie Smith. *Slam for Life: The Story of a Girl's AAU Basketball Team*. Pittsburgh: Rosedog Books, 2011.

Sokolove, Michael. *Warrior Girls: Protecting Our Daughters against the Injury Epidemic in Women's Sports*. New York: Simon & Schuster, 2008.

Spock, Benjamin. *Baby and Child Care*. New York: Duell, Sloan and Pearce, 1946.

I

WHY IS THE COACH'S SON ALWAYS THE QUARTERBACK?

An Expansion of Gladwell's *Outliers*

The obsession with "success," especially as it pertains to the accumulation of wealth, fame, and power, is seen through the public's taste in reality television where "real housewives" compete with celebrity this and celebrity that and all involve people who bask in the trappings of their usually opulent lifestyles. This obsession with wealth, fame, and power plays perhaps an equally significant role in sports in our society. When our obsession with the trappings of "success" intersects with our obsession for sports, and that obsession results in our involvement with youth sports, all indeed may be lost.

Those of us who love sports might suggest that our obsessions are healthy ones, for after all, there are worse things we could be doing than volunteering our time to coach our children's teams. Or for those of us not so inclined to give our time and talents (real or perceived) to coaching, we frequently still engage in periphery activities related to our children's sports, from driving several teammates to games to providing snacks for them after the games have ended. For some, attendance at a child's sporting events might cover the years from preschool through college and might shape family weekends, family finances, and even major family decisions. All of this obsessing might lend itself to the argument that the involvement that many parents have with their child's sports borders on the unhealthy and the harmful. Beauty may indeed be in the eye of the beholder when it comes to the fine-line distinction between appropriate supportive relationships and unhealthy hovering in the level of parental participation in their children's sporting lives. Garrison Keillor has become famous for his books, recordings, and even a movie in which his *Prairie Home Companion* radio show was depicted. In these forums he often refers to "Lake Wobegon," a small bucolic Minnesota town in which the children are all "above average." While Keillor uses humor to poke fun at parents who, sometimes inappropriately, laud their children's accomplishments, his point seems appropriate in this context in which parents view their children's athletic prowess as consistently "above average."

If parents quite naturally often live their lives under the rules of the "Lake Wobegon effect," in which all children are "above average," and they view their children as exceptional, then their viewpoints toward how much playing time their own children should receive and their criticisms of coaching, refereeing, and so forth, become, or at least may become, unnaturally skewed, and thus harmful. Parents sometimes might benefit from the same realities that face our children as their levels of competition increase, and they come to recognize that their talents may indeed be "above average" in many contexts, but quite average or even below in other contexts. We will discuss, in a later chapter, the ongoing trend of "moving" young athletes into other venues where they will face higher competition and receive better coaching and have access to better facilities. While there is danger in that, of course—and our discussion will feature much of that potential danger and the implications for "growing up too fast" that accompany many of those moves—there may also be value for parents in recognizing that some of their expectations and beliefs are simply unreasonable. That "exceptional" child who excels and dominates on the basketball court or the baseball field in his hometown may come to face other exceptional young athletes when they travel, and just as that may increase their level of play, it may also be an effective way of tempering their parents' expectations. Measuring oneself against the competition available is pretty standard procedure in most of our adult lives. Recognizing that better competition might exist elsewhere and more and better work might be required in different contexts may be a valuable use of our time.

The sport of golf provides an easy example. Golf courses have "ratings" so that the golfer might judge his or her round beyond the measure of his or her score. Some courses are more difficult than others. Some competition is simply better than other competition. If all we ever do is play "easy" courses, our scores would necessarily be inflated, and our opinions of our game might subsequently be wildly inflated. While we may be pretty good on our home course, we may wilt when we face the pressures associated with a more difficult golf course. The same can be true of those who play other sports, and particularly when those sports involve team competition. Measuring oneself by one's competition seems quite natural; so too should improving oneself by increasing that level of competition.

Many of our best athletes no doubt are considered our best athletes because of their outstanding and "outlying" abilities that transcend the more common abilities that many possess; still, that ability is not always the exclusive reason for "success." There is another powerful reason that many of these athletes have become elite, and that reason lies at least in part in a rather "unnatural selection" process that separated them from their "less able" peers at relatively young ages.

"UNNATURAL SELECTION"

While sports sometimes becomes close to religion with regard to the passion that is generated, the notion of "unnatural selection" isn't meant to trample upon anyone's beliefs, but rather to suggest that conventional wisdom often propels beliefs into accepted facts. The "fact" that my kid is better than your kid should be a much harder sell than merely that same "belief." Unfortunately, in youth sports we often create our own facts and our own self-fulfilling prophecies when we allow beliefs to become translated into facts. Getting a coach to "believe" that one five- or six- or seven-year-old is more athletically skilled than another becomes relatively easily translated into the later reality, when we can see with our own eyes that those athletes at the skilled positions are indeed simply more skilled than those who aren't in those positions. But how did they get there? How did they *really* get there?

Malcolm Gladwell's best seller *Outliers* begins by examining the question of what makes certain people truly stand out in their chosen fields. Our research and perceptions seem to validate much of what Gladwell suggests but also goes beyond to further explore why some, even at a very young age, are perhaps not so much "outliers" as they are, at least to some degree, the "chosen ones."

The title of this chapter suggests that being "chosen" as the quarterback of one's seven-year-old Pop Warner team often depends upon factors beyond one's ability to throw the ball. Similarly the little boy or girl who is assigned the "quarterback-like" position of point guard on the basketball team often gets that assignment based on something more than a natural affinity to lead his or her teammates because of his or her innate skill set and/or his or her ability to drive to the hoop or make the perfect pass to an open teammate. Is there something more that separates that child from his or her peers, and is that something more a factor than we have been reluctant to admit exists? In many ways we believe it is the elephant in the room when it comes to youth sports. The "chosen" athletes necessarily are separated, often literally from those who are not so revered and almost always figuratively, in the sense that they are separated in their own and others' perceptions. That separation at such a young age may defeat a lot about what is good about youth sports.

> One of the best things about youth sports is that they are participatory—children who play are actively involved. Yet even by the time children are nine or ten, there is a push toward the selection of the "best" athletes, who get the chance to keep playing, while the "not so good" athletes are discouraged from playing or encouraged to watch the good athletes. (Murphy 1999, 35)

While a child must possess a minimum threshold of athletic ability to be considered for the elite positions and teams, what actually separates them from several children who cross that initial threshold, but for a variety of reasons, never really get full inclusion into elite athletic status? If, for example, a group of seven-year-olds can essentially throw the football in a similar fashion, with similar arm strength and with similar control, who then becomes the "chosen one"? What factors, beyond obvious athletic prowess, determines one's place within the pecking order of youth sports and how does that pecking order at a young age lead into similar "career" development into middle school, high school, and beyond? When baseball and softball teams are forming, how does the coach decide who gets instruction in pitching and who get instruction in the infield versus the outfield? Depending upon the opportunities presented to children and the areas in which they grow up, there may even be the occasional retired major leaguer or at least retired scout or baseball executive who gives of their time and instructs the players, but typically they would only come on occasion and only after the selection process has been made by the coach. Once again, who gets the best instruction? The children already chosen to receive that instruction are the ones who will benefit, while others are relegated to watch from the sidelines or from the outfield.

If *Outliers* contributes to the popular mythology that presumes meritocracy at least insofar as the most talented child on the team will play quarterback, then it is at least worthy of our consideration to suggest that there may be other significant factors at play beyond ability. This premise does not suggest that Gladwell's points regarding the skills that a few possess as well as the drive that a relatively few possess in relation to the rest of us are wrong. Gladwell points out, for example, that the young athletes who are chosen for the elite teams then necessarily get more and better practice times, more and better coaching, and better teammates and competition (2008). In essence the chosen children get greater access and better opportunities, creating in effect a self-fulfilling prophecy that those originally perceived as the "best" do in fact usually become the "best."

Beyond the increased practice time and better coaching, we're also suggesting that the "initial selection process" in which the seven-year-old is assigned the role of quarterback is at least as important as his or her ability. The recognition of the importance of the "initial selection process" adds another variable to Gladwell's equation as it might pertain to youth sports. This also allows coaches the "freedom" to be the reigning experts in the field of athletic ability, as given the time and the resources devoted to certain individuals, they have tremendous power to shape any outsider's conclusions about the abilities of individual athletes. In other words, since we don't attend practice and we don't actually see the "selection process" at work, we are left to view the finished result: a (hopefully) finely tuned skilled athlete who seems to excel beyond his or her peers. When we attend the game, we see a talented athlete playing quarterback, which then justifies the coach's initial decision to choose the athlete as the quarterback. We could question the coach, I suppose, but usually when one questions an "expert" the experience leaves the questioner somewhat humbled . . . or worse. Thus, we simply accept the expert's take on the subject. It's not unlike some of the head scratching we all do when we view political pundits on television telling us something that doesn't necessarily seem inherently correct, but to question their judgment would be to suggest we know more than the expert, and not only would that suggest a certain egomania on our parts, but a naïveté that is beneath us all. Thus, we remain quiet and accept the expertise of our experts. Being labeled an "expert" as you can see, and as is true in almost any vocation, is a good gig, and experts in youth sports are the coaches.

This concept of the "initial selection process" nicely parallels other "labeling" theories from criminology to sociology, in which people who are labeled in one way or another often feel intense pressure to either live up to or down to the labels attached. We speak of social capital and building social capital in this same regard. As professors, we've suggested to students that it is important to build social capital or social equity on campus. If you want people to "cut you some slack" if and when you underperform, it is always best to have built a reputation of high performance so any potential underperformance is viewed as an aberration and thus not worthy of any long-term analysis. When we look at that concept in the world of sports, any number of examples can be used, in which star quarterbacks can have bad or "underperforming" games, but there is nary a hint of benching them long term, as their performance was seen as an aberration, and probably justly so. In contrast, however, when the rookie or the backup steps in, he better perform at a high level pretty quickly, as he simply hasn't built up equity that will protect him should he have a bad game, and thus, his benching may occur more quickly and be more prolonged. The danger of being labeled as a "career backup" rather than as a starter is very real.

In kids' sports, the same is true, as the "chosen" players can have bad games, but the "lesser"—or those labeled as "lesser"—had better perform at a high level when given the chance, or they may not be given the chance again. For children in sports, not being among the chosen is truly a daunting proposition. The pressure that is placed upon those who barely get into the game, to perform at a high level once they are in so that the coach notices their worth, likely contributes, in most cases, to a lack of success. As if the world weren't unfair enough: the kids who get to play get to make mistakes, while the kids who barely get in have no such opportunity to make mistakes.

At the risk of speaking out of both sides of our mouths, some of this is purely understandable. Once a person establishes a reputation, that reputation endures. Why wouldn't a coach pull Michael Jordan or Kobe Bryant out of the game after he'd missed his first five or even his first ten shots? The answer, of course, is because they are Michael Jordan and Kobe Bryant—they may make their next ten shots—and thus it would border on the insane to pull them before they establish their rhythm and get into the flow of the game. But what if the bench player missed his first five shots? Would the coach be as forgiving? Of course not, and thus, that player in that position had better not miss his first five shots, or maybe even his first one or two shots, as he knows very well that he won't be left in the game to find his game, and the pressure mounts accordingly. Probably most of us who have children of a certain age and who have attended any variety of sporting events have seen the struggles of the child who is finally put into the game and then feels so much pressure to perform well and right away, that he or she simply "forces" every shot, or otherwise feels so much pressure to perform that he or she simply doesn't perform well. Some of those kids have already been asked to be "merely a role player" and to get the ball to the "stars" and basically get out of their way. All of which adds to the pressure the "lesser" player feels and the need for that player to somehow make an impression in situations where making an impression becomes almost impossible. You can almost feel the pain as they are taken out of the game after a minute or two, and the coach is vindicated in believing that indeed, just as he or she knew all along, the player simply wasn't good enough to play.

So why is the coach's child often perceived as one of the better players on the team? As a result, why does it become only "natural" that he or she should logically play the most coveted positions? Is it as Gladwell suggests of his "outliers," that "they are invariably the beneficiaries of hidden advantages and extraordinary opportunities and cultural legacies that allow them to learn and work hard and make sense of the world in ways others cannot" (2008, 19)? Or is that a concept that applies only for very successful people and bears little relevance to children's sports? In essence, are the coach's children really "outliers" at an early age, or is it more relevant that they are the coach's children, and thus will be consciously or unconsciously favored at that very first practice? While coaches do exist who place their sons or daughters in the nonelite positions on the field, more often than not, the coach places his or her child in a coveted position.

We often hear about cultural, physical, and social capital and how people benefit from that capital. An example can be seen in Robert Putnam's *Bowling Alone* (2001), which discusses the concept of "social capital."

> Just as a screwdriver (physical capital) or a college education (human capital) can increase productivity (both individual and collective), so too can social contacts affect the productivity of individuals and groups . . . social capital refers to connections among individuals—social networks and the norms of reciprocity and trustworthiness that arise from them. (Putnam 2001, 19)

It has been said that education is less what Horace Mann envisioned as the "great equalizer of the conditions of men" and more a reproduction of social inequality, as it sometimes proportions academic success to the amount of cultural capital that a family possesses. We suggest that "athletic capital" has similar qualities that benefit individuals in similar ways, with sports reproducing and even enhancing greater inequality.

In accordance with what we associate with other forms of capital, athletic capital considers whether there is the means and knowledge to invest in the child's athletic participation and performance. The family of the young athlete must have the financial resources, knowledge, and time to support their child's athletic development. (A caveat to this is a child who truly excels at a sport that is popular in mainstream American culture, for example, basketball, where there is now external financial support and mentoring for individuals who show promise to go to a Division I basketball program or "go pro.") Generally, athletic promise must be accompanied by opportunities to refine that promise. For example, along with physical coordination, there often is access to support for the child looking to enhance his or her abilities in order to gain "athletic capital." Resources to play in tournaments and stay in hotels in distant places and attend a variety of "camps" intended to improve play and improve visibility are necessary in order to make the most of whatever "athletic capital" is inherently available. It "takes money to make money" is a truism we all accept; so too does it take athletic capital to make athletic capital. The more one has, the more likely it can be enhanced. We begin to consider the implications of the concept of "athletic capital" in this context; we more fully examine it ahead in chapter 3.

For a family there most likely needs to be at least one parent who has a history and/or interest in sports and thinks participation in athletics is important to a child, as exercise, character building, or advancement, or some combination of all of those. When there is a history of parental sports participation, it more naturally follows that the parents will encourage opportunities for a child to participate. It also often naturally follows that such a parent will become the son or daughter's coach. Parents will understand and support practice time and be more willing to put in their own time to help, whether that is on the field of play or carpooling or making team dinners. This access to support also often includes actual involvement in practice at an early age. Throwing the ball around in the park or backyard is a form of parental involvement that some kids have and others do not, and for some kids, that throwing the ball around becomes an early unorganized form of practice. The role that nature versus nurture plays in the development of a child has long been debated. When a child becomes an adult who engages in criminal behavior, for example, there is constant analysis of how his or her parents influenced that outcome and how much biology simply took over. Likewise, when an adult develops medical problems, doctors who do their due diligence examine that patient's family history to find the influence of genetic factors in disease formation. We believe that children who are read to at an early age are more prone to develop a love of reading than those who were not. It would seem to follow that children whose parents value or place emphasis upon sports would be more likely to produce children who share that emphasis. Readers of this who watch television may be familiar with the recent Volkswagen commercial in which a father and son are in the front yard playing catch: in the spot, the father has on obvious complete lack of athletic ability and is unable to throw the ball anywhere near the son, and the son's return throws are no better. We cut to the new beautiful car in the driveway, and the voiceover announcer expresses gladness that while it appears that the father will not be passing any athletic ability down to the son, he can still pass on the car someday. Humor and commercialism aside, the point is well made and we think should be well taken: that passing athletic ability and an interest in sports to our children is as natural as the passing of other traits (and other shortcomings).

Today, participating in youth sports requires a significant investment of family resources, most particularly in the form of money and time. Therefore a family who wants their child or children to participate in sports has to have the financial resources to support them. There are often fees for public school participation in a given sport. In addition, for many sports, like basketball, football, lacrosse, softball, and baseball, the player is required to purchase the team shoes. To play golf, students must have their own clubs and golf balls. Swimmers often must join their local YMCA or some other facility, and that involves winter and summer swimming fees. If your child chooses or is chosen to compete outside of school, for example on a traveling team, there is a fee, which covers the uniforms and all other costs such as umpires and field rentals. Also the family, or at least one parent or adult, has to travel with the young player, and that involves hotel and restaurant costs of hundreds of dollars per season.

In addition to considering the material costs, there is also an assumption that an adult in the child's life can organize this effort and can take time away from work in order to manage the logistics. The young athlete needs to be dropped off and picked up at practices and games and supported during games. Parents may be expected to supply food or host a team dinner, contribute to coaches' gifts and spirit campaigns, and so on. The family not only must be willing to invest the parent's time and money, but there are financial and time repercussions for the entire family as well. "Parents get sucked in, caught up. They've signed away their entire spring or their summer or winter vacations before they even ask what their family will need to give up in order for their children to play youth sports" (Bigelow et al. 2001, 79).

This ability to free up time to support a child's interest in sports and to spare the resources to put into it is not available to every child. Not only is there the time commitment on the part of the parent, but there is also the time commitment on the part of the child him- or herself. We know of many instances in which teenagers simply do not have time to get a summer job, as they are far too committed to various summer training programs, camps for their various sports, and travel to faraway tournaments. Obviously, as with other choices that are more real for some than they are for others, the choice not to get a job and make some money isn't available to everyone. Some young people need a job in order to have money to spend on necessities and to have some fun, while other young people do not need to spend their time on such trivial pursuits as working in relatively menial jobs to make some spending money. Parenting issues abound, as usual, concerning summer jobs for teenagers: Should a teenager have a job in order to teach them responsibility, the value of money, the reward of hard work, and so on? Or is "forcing" one's teenager to work limiting their practice time and their ability to attend the many athletic programs that their nonworking peers are attending? Parental guilt is a possibility both ways, of course. Certainly the emphasis placed upon organized sports in this manner is yet another change in society, as the notion of allowing one's teenager to specialize only on sports and not on work—or as our grandparents might have said: only on *play*, and not on work—would've been irresponsible parenting not that long ago. The time commitment involved in working has created in some sports circles this simple fact: a young person is so committed time-wise to training and to camps and other sports-related ventures, that they simply have no time for work.

The idea that having a job and the responsibilities that go with it, or even having chores that must be performed around the house, as a means of instilling character and an appropriate work ethic that will assist the child as he or she develops through life, is being lost. This also contributes to a loss of community in the neighborhoods in which we live, as children who might otherwise rake leaves, mow lawns, and otherwise interact with their neighbors, as a means of making some money and/or helping their neighbors, are now far too busy with their organized sports and sports-related activities to find the time to engage with the neighbors or to worry about making money. Many parents, now thoroughly obsessed with college scholarships for their children, view this as a necessary consequence as they weigh their own costs/benefits analysis of their children's involvement in sports. Why should parents worry about a child making a few bucks spending money, if that takes time away from their efforts to gain a college scholarship that will benefit them far more financially? "Elitism" has really crept into this sporting culture, as many of those vying (at least in their minds) for college scholarships view the idea of working for minimum wage not as a character-building experience, but as a waste of time.

Gladwell (2008) talks about access and playing time in terms of NHL players (or access to computer labs in reference to Bill Gates) and similarly, we have found, at least anecdotally, that a coach's child is allotted more playing time than other members of the team. Further, the child of a coach is more likely to be around or partake in discussions that center on sports. For example, the child is privy to frequent dinner conversations and family members who watch sporting events on television. Sports very likely are part of the family's everyday discussion, which holds value for that family and establishes for the child that being able to participate is rewarded. As with cultural capital, sports and the values surrounding sports become part of the fabric of the family and therefore are inculcated into the child's value system.

As with the other forms of capital, athletic capital does not stand alone; social capital complements athletic capital: who you know and the range of networking contacts also contributes to athletic capital. Young people's athletic prowess plays a role in their getting picked for teams or in what order they get picked, and who they or their parents know may influence those choices. Today youth teams are rarely randomly assigned, or if they are, it is only at the youngest levels. While this is less true in the public schools, it nevertheless does happen and it is definitely a factor in youth sports outside of the school system. Parents/adults (especially true for the coach) control the teams, tournaments, and leagues. Teams are formed around the coaches and who the coaches know affects who they pick for "their" teams and how much playing time the players get. A coach seems more likely to let a player push through mistakes and leave that player in the game if there is a connection to the player's family. Being the coach's son or daughter can mean even greater advantages in terms of getting more playing time, including a greater likelihood of being a "starter" and being kept in the game even after making mistakes on the field. This allows the player more trial and error time and more coaching time—most importantly this allows him or her the advantage of learning from mistakes and how to correct them. This also allows the confidence building that accompanies making mistakes and being allowed to play through them in contrast to the child who makes mistakes and sits on the bench as a result.

Whatever it is, it would seem that the inherent advantage of being the coach's child has now become part of the popular culture and conventional wisdom of athletics. One cannot watch a televised sporting event (or so it seems to us) without the announcers making note of the fact that the point guard or quarterback or pitcher grew up as the son of a coach. Newspapers and websites also frequently refer to the phenomenon of the coach's son:

> You might say Gardner-Webb University quarterback Stan Doolittle has been groomed for this moment. The Ninety-Six, S.C. native has played and studied the quarterback position his entire life. That goes with being the son of a coach. (Ford 2009)

Surely some of the coach's apparent athletic prowess must have been passed on to the prodigy (though seemingly if that were more important, we'd hear of more cases in which professional athletes parented other professional athletes). Given that it is relatively rare that a professional athlete has a child who becomes a professional athlete him- or herself, this chapter has instead focused upon the phenomenon of athletic capital in which the young athlete begins to build upon early success and continue to expand that capital and watch it grow.

If practice makes perfect, it would seem that getting a number of repetitions in practice would greatly help one's potential for future success. So perhaps it only makes sense that the "glamour" positions are often held by coaches' kids; after all, the coach selected the positions of the players, and while there are no doubt thousands of cases in which personal biases did not impact the placement of a son or daughter, there are surely thousands of others in which personal bias did.

All things being equal—which among seven-year-olds is often the case—with limited attention spans and limited physical gifts, why wouldn't the coach put his or her son or daughter into the glamour positions? Only in clear-cut cases where another seven-year-old is exceptional (and by definition that shouldn't happen often) would it be noticed if injustice occurred, by favoring one child over another with superior athletic skills. In the majority of cases, placing the child of a coach in a glamour position at an early age might create a self-fulfilling prophecy, insofar as the child gets the repetitions necessary and the confidence is placed in him or her such that after a few years, he or she becomes the obvious choice to play that position. Any controversy that might have arisen is quashed by the nature of practice and repetition. The confidence of the coach and the accompanying expanded practice time and expanded capital at that favored position contribute to the making of a successful athlete. It takes only a relatively short time to realize the results of all of this: that the player selected has in fact, in short order, become the best at that position, and to change and give another athlete a chance to compete at that position would be folly at that point, thereby fulfilling the prophecy that the coach/father really did know best. Without overemphasizing this point, the parent who brings forth his or her child as a seven-year-old to begin the process of playing football or basketball or baseball or whatever, isn't really expecting the first couple of days of practice to shape the long-term career of that child. Unfortunately, those expectations of simplicity may be misplaced. Our experience suggests that perhaps the parent should be more prepared to accept that indeed those first few days are actually critical in determining whether that child is ever going to have the opportunity to play a glamour position. Remember the old joke: How do you get to Carnegie Hall? Practice. How do you get to be quarterback? Practice. But how do you get that practice in a team sport? You have to be selected by the coach to start taking the repetitions that create a quarterback, and if you're not chosen early, those repetitions are going to go to somebody else.

There are vastly more significant implications than merely the pride (often misplaced anyway) of a parent who wants his or her son or daughter to achieve some level of glory on the football field or the basketball court. The more serious implications involve the child. The child who isn't selected, and who becomes a "benchwarmer" before they are ten years old, must endure that label and, as a natural consequence, sometimes makes a perfectly rational decision to give up on a given sport before anyone (including the child) actually has any real idea whether or not they can achieve success at it. The "unnatural selection" not only allows for some to be chosen, but obviously, it also creates the corollary effect: that some will be left behind. Many children stay with their sports, whether for the love of the game or at the behest of their parents, and some eventually might even get a chance to play, but many others opt out relatively early, whether to save face or to simply turn to other activities in which the rewards might be more attainable. But how many of those children who weren't given good positions to play, or who were left on the end of the bench, would actually have been good players had they been given a chance?

As this chapter was being written, the New York Knickerbockers of the NBA were experiencing the "Jeremy Lin phenomenon," in which an end of the bench guy finally got his chance to play and responded by setting records for scoring in his first five NBA starts. Lin has since moved on to the Houston Rockets, and as with most news/sports stories, what was dominating all the headlines for a week or two seems light-years away now; but the point remains current and inspirational for those who aren't "the chosen ones." This isn't to suggest that the Jeremy Lin story is a common one, but his reality might encourage those who aren't the chosen ones, and might provide a cautionary tale to the rest of us who might quickly label those who don't get the opportunity to play as those who don't *deserve* to play. Sports are often labeled a true meritocracy insofar as we think that those who fail get benched and those who succeed get to play. This label, in our view, may be overstated, and examples like Jeremy Lin would suggest that while it may be closer to a true merit system than other social systems and even our economic system, it still isn't all that close to a pure merit system. All of which may go some distance toward explaining why it is that "the coach's son is always the quarterback."

WORKS CITED

Bigelow, Bob, Tom Moroney, and Linda Hall. *Just Let the Kids Play: How to Stop Other Adults from Ruining Your Child's Fun and Success in Youth Sports*. Deerfield Beach, FL: Health Communications, Inc., 2001.

Ford, A. "QB Doolittle Takes Leadership Role at GWU in Stride." *Shelby Star*, last modified September 18, 2009. http://www.shelbystar.com/articles/quarterback-41795-doolittle-life.html.

Gladwell, Malcolm. *Outliers: The Story of Success*. New York: Little, Brown, and Company, 2008.

Keillor, Garrison. *Lake Wobegon Days*. New York: Viking Press, 1985.

Murphy, Shane. *The Cheers and the Tears: A Healthy Alternative to the Dark Side of Youth Sports Today*. San Francisco: Jossey-Bass Publishers, 1999.

Putnam, Robert D. *Bowling Alone: The Collapse and Revival of American Community*. New York: Simon & Schuster, 2001.

2

LITTLE LEAGUE PARENTS

The Fine Line between Healthy Obsession and Unhealthy Behavior

Teaching our children to manipulate the outcome of events, take advantage of opportunities, and engage in uncivil behavior is becoming all too common in our culture. The influence that "helicopter parents" have, not only upon their own children but upon American culture, is becoming a pervasive subject in academic literature and mainstream dialogue. By examining aspects of behavior displayed by parents at Little League baseball games, Amateur Athletic Union (AAU) basketball games, and other youth sporting events, we hope to continue and expand the discussion about the perceived increase in incivility in our society. There may very well be practical implications of questionable parental behavior that transcend merely another example of incivility in our society.

Our interviews with college coaches, as well as conversations with those connected with AAU basketball as both coaches and recruiters, suggest quite openly that coaches do watch the behavior of parents and are reluctant to involve themselves with players whose parents would appear to be high maintenance. Naturally, for players who are exceptional, many flaws are overlooked: grades in school are seemingly less important for the truly gifted athlete, just as behavior issues generally are seemingly less important for those with genuine potential. But for the marginal or for those who are being compared to others of similar ability for a coach's affection, the behavioral issues of their parents in the stands can become a genuine factor in how attractive they might appear to those coaches who otherwise might have great interest in them. Overbearing parents can be such a turn-off to college coaches, that in some cases, even skilled players are not recruited, as the coach is probably correctly concerned that too much effort will be required to keep those parents happy and off his or her back.

There may very well be a connection between behavior of parents at Little League games (or other venues in which hyperinvolved parents make their presence known for good and ill) and the development of children who through adolescence and even young adulthood display characteristics consistent with the roles played by their parents. As college professors, we are all too familiar with helicopter parents who send their sons and daughters away to school, but nevertheless remain able and willing to manage their day-to-day affairs. Calls from parents to professors, to administrators, to student service personnel, and presumably to roommates and resident advisors are becoming far from rare occurrences. It would seem that a parent's inability to let go isn't just a phenomenon when they send their children off to Little League fields to be in the care of coaches, but remains very real even as they send their adult children off to college. Those of us working in colleges and universities see this hovering behavior in a variety of contexts. We have both been involved in student visits in which the students have no questions (and sometimes seemingly no interest in attending our school or learning about our programs), but their parents are asking numerous questions that would seem to be vastly more appropriate for their children to be asking.

Helicopter parents appear in the headlines of news sources:

- "Hovering Parents Need to Step Back at College Time," *Health Minute*, February 2008
- "Helicopter Parents Cross All Ages, Social Lines," usatoday.com, April 3, 2007
- "When Parents Hover over Kids' Job Search," msnbc.com, November 7, 2006

The term "helicopter parents" is a phrase that has been defined in popular culture as consisting of those parents who rush to prevent any harm or failure that might befall their children by hovering closely by and essentially attempting to control any and all outcomes. While that may be a rather generic definition of the term, and one that certainly applies to educators who receive phone calls from Mom or Dad about a son or daughter, it also applies more and more to those parents who hover around youth activities, and particularly for our purposes, Little League fields. Helicopter parents, in this context, attempt to influence and control the outcomes of children's games and that may explain why we, as college professors who see these kids a decade later, still must often deal with parents who have honed their skills in manipulating others on Little League fields. If a parent on a Little League field, or a parent who watches his or her son or daughter perform in the orchestra or in a theatrical production, has had some success in influencing bene-fits that have accrued to the child, then why should we be surprised when these parents attempt, years later, to make certain that benefits accrue to their now-college-aged child? It is becoming increasingly popular in some school districts for principals to notify students of their class assignments only immediately prior to taking a vacation, in much the same way that a political figure might announce some embarrassing news or data on a holiday or some other day in which the media might be preoccupied or uninterested. To announce class assignments too early is to invite a horde of parents to request (in some cases demand) changes that allow them their own choice of teachers or classmates. The difficulty that school administrators face in making these seemingly arbitrary decisions has increased exponentially as more and more par-ents feel comfortable in making their own beliefs known.

Many of us grew up in "simpler" times when, even if we weren't thrilled with the assignment of a given teacher or the separation of best friends, we could be certain that our parents were not about to lift a finger to "help" us change these outcomes. "You'll make new friends" or "That teacher will be fine" has been replaced in many homes with "Don't worry; we'll take care of it" or "How could the principal do this? We will call him immediately and see to it that a change is made."

The influence of helicopter parenting has changed the way in which many children see the world around them and the way in which many parents interact with those in positions of power or influence. The contrast between what once was considered appropriate and acceptable parental behavior and what is now considered indifference or a lack of caring is stark. That contrast is easily viewed in the world of youth sports.

Attending Little League baseball games has always been a study in contrasts. We might contrast those kids with already obvious skills against those with little athletic ability and those with a passionate desire to play with those more interested in the flora, the fauna, and the occasional passing airplane. But perhaps the starkest contrast is between those parents concerned with their children's enjoyment of the game and those already bent upon laying a foundation for their child's fame, fortune, and what must seem to them an already inevitable college scholarship.

As we write this chapter, with topics seeded in our own interest in sports, and baseball particularly, we find ourselves navigating the fine line between our own perceived healthy obsession and what some might consider a baseball addiction. Much of the discussion in this section will focus upon what is problematic about Little League. We acknowledge that despite our knowledge of many of the problems inherent in today's sporting environment, we still simply cannot give up our interest in baseball, nor would we want our children to walk away from what might become a lifelong and, we like to think, healthy obsession with the game. The power of being a fan and the need to follow "your" team is a very real phenomenon for many people. Television networks' recognition of the obsessed fan and that fan's need to follow his or her team has made possible the many sports programming options that allow for those of us who live far away from our childhood teams to pay premium prices to remain loyal and follow our beloved teams. It also somewhat explains why the passionate fan sometimes takes vicarious credit for the successes of his or her favorite team—"I can't believe *we* won!"—while they disassociate themselves from failures—"I can't believe *they* lost." The misplaced, or at least overly intense, passion is seen in some fans' willingness to physically fight the fans of other teams, which has resulted in serious injuries to fans in certain stadiums. Discretion being the better part of valor also forces reluctance on the part of some fans to even wear the colors of their favorite team in opposing stadiums for fear of being targeted in a way far more perilous than what might have simply once been an amusing taunt.

The interest/obsession many people have with sports generally, and baseball in particular, may also stem as much from our remembrances of our sporting heroes from our youth as it does from our own experiences with a bat and ball. Many of us have experiences on Little League baseball fields. Some of us can remember those experiences vividly, just as we remember our varying levels of ability as we learned the game. Those memories are, no doubt, impacted as much by what happened around the field just as surely as what happened on the field. The quality of baseball being played was probably pretty much the same everywhere with each team sporting excellent players who could eventually move up the childhood baseball ladder and maybe even achieve some level of success in high school and beyond. Each team also featured lesser-skilled players who struggled to achieve any level of success at even the most basic aspects of the game, and as time passed it often became apparent that their interest in the game stemmed more from their parents' requirements than their own desires. Still others, and probably most, fell somewhere in between: spacing quality play with inept play and generally achieving a level of mediocrity that allowed enjoyment but not exactly total confidence. Mediocrity generally meant that most of the players could make a good baseball play . . . sometimes, just as they could make a very poor baseball play . . . sometimes; it was difficult to completely count on any ten- to twelve-year-old acting as a model of consistency, both on and off the field. Generally, we wouldn't expect young people of that age to consistently do the right thing and consistently live their lives without making errors. It might serve us well to consider that larger construct as we examine Little League baseball and youth sports more generally.

Perhaps that was then, but what about now? Ours is not a society that rewards or often even accepts mediocrity. Expectations of parents and coaches often pressure young children into avoidance of mediocrity in one way or the other. If the players are talented, they are encouraged to practice more, dedicate themselves to their craft, and otherwise forsake many other things in order to move beyond that large gray zone known as mediocrity. If, in contrast, the players are not talented, they are often soon encouraged in a far different direction. Encouragement, in fact, might be a strange choice of words to describe a process in which the young people are encouraged to focus upon something else. There is nothing wrong with choosing something else, they are told;

after all, there is something for everyone. What is wrong, seemingly at least, is to be mediocre or even worse. There is simply no place in the sports world for those people. Obviously, there is no room for mediocrity in professional sports, but on Little League fields? Shouldn't a certain acceptance of mediocrity be a part of the Little League process, as it should be in all childhood pursuits?

It may be appropriate here to add that, in many cases, the "encouragement" to choose a different sport, while invoking great sadness for the young athlete at the time, often brings with it some serious silver linings. Many of us could share anecdotes from our own towns in which baseball players cut from the team decided to run track instead, and ended up having great success in that sport, including, in some cases, even college scholarships. The same has been true in other sports, as well, where budding football players are encouraged to play another sport, and they become collegiate lacrosse stars. These anecdotes are merely that, anecdotes. Still, they do suggest that the fine line separating victory from defeat in sports also separates failure in one sport from success in another.

On-the-field mediocrity is one thing, and our collective disdain for it has become central to our inability to accept playing for fun. Somewhere we seemed to have gotten ahead of ourselves. We seem to expect a level of competence that for many children simply isn't there . . . yet anyway. Rather than wait for them to achieve that level of competence, we often simply cut our losses and encourage them to pursue something that they would be good at. Such belief systems have led to a caste system when it comes to athletes. Interestingly, perhaps, many folks poised in the art of self-improvement might suggest that the only way to succeed is to not be afraid to fail. (Those of us who work on college campuses are quite familiar with this standard theme so prevalent in many commencement addresses.) But while we seem to accept such platitudes for our graduating seniors, we seem reluctant to accept similar beliefs with regard to younger students. We seem to be moving away from any allowance or even tolerance for failure in the athletic realm, as we don't allow our children to fail . . . at least for long. If they fail, they should probably move on to something else at which they can succeed. It is as if the old adage of "try and try again" has been displaced by something more akin to "try, succeed, or move on."

How does the role of parents play into what seems like a new approach to youth sports? When many children are born, especially boys, they are given their first baseball glove, ball, and perhaps even a jersey representing the parents' favorite team. Does the pressure to perform athletically begin immediately? Parents sometimes compete with other parents when it comes to a child's first steps, first words, or even first effective toilet experience. If competition can occur over these common developments, it is rather easy to imagine how our competitive natures seem to take over when a child shows some level of ability in any skill, let alone the competitive world of sports.

The role of parents in the development of their children can hardly be denied. From teaching our children to tie their shoes, take care of their own hygiene, and handle day-to-day adventures, we progress into teaching them how to handle themselves when out of our direct supervision. Some interesting situations arise as children begin handling themselves on their own and participating in organized sports. Children have, of course, a variety of different home experiences. For some, their first organized sport has come after many sessions in the backyard playing catch or involving themselves in other sporting activities. For others, and particularly for those whose parents never considered themselves athletic, their first sporting experiences do occur in the company of strangers. The variety of experiences prior to that first organized sporting experience leads to a variety of experiences at that first organized sport. That variety allows for the on-the-field activities to be both interesting to watch and fun to be a part of, but what occurs off the field and around the field during the games perhaps provides us with more lasting memories, and possibly more important lessons. Experiences with Little League allow many children to become interested in the game, but few become passionate about it. Many parents, it would seem, begin the process by wanting their children to simply try something new and/or have fun, but somewhere along the way, some of these parents become obsessed with winning, success, and the future potential of their young athletes. How and why does this happen? Is fun for children the same as fun for their parents when it comes to youth sports? When does the appropriate need to seek what is best for one's children and the proper focus upon fun, give way to a need to drive the child toward a level of perfection that may be difficult, if not impossible, to attain?

Some parents seem to have crossed over the fine line from a relatively healthy interest in their children's games toward a full-scale obsession with their child's performance. Our experiences suggest that for every healthy parent/child relationship in which the parent cheers for the child's team and wants what the child wants, there is an unhealthy relationship in which the parent is driven solely by the level of success they perceive for their child. Whether this is catharsis or a simple admission, parents sometimes will acknowledge that they themselves take a loss or a poor performance by their child much harder than the child him- or herself. While the child may make a critical error or strikeout at clutch time, and then join the team for ice cream or otherwise put the failure behind them, the parents may literally and figuratively lose sleep over how best to put their child in a better position to succeed the next time. Is that healthy? When does wanting your child to improve his or her performance begin to interfere with the child's actual life? How can we be sure that little Timmy or Susie really wants to excel in a given sport, and how can we be sure that their motivations aren't based more upon wanting to please their parents? While we congratulate and even laud the parents of our Olympic champions and pro athletes who drove the children to practice (both literally and figuratively again), we might use caution when we consider how many other parents did the same driving but didn't end up in the same place. What about all those athletes who simply didn't measure up? When did their parents recognize that the college scholarship wasn't forthcoming or that the pro career was simply not going to materialize? Perhaps even more importantly, when did the child realize the same, and did the child even envision that college scholarship as a goal in the same way that his or her parents did? Did the child simply want to play for the pleasure of playing and/or the camaraderie of his or her teammates?

It's unlikely that a typical seven- or eight-year-old gives much thought to a college scholarship, but it is not uncommon to have a conversation with their parents in which that thought process has already taken root. If the parents (wrongly or rightly) perceive that their child is a gifted athlete based on the performances they see in front of their eyes, then it is even easier to understand how the end goal for the parents might differ from the end goal of the child (which was probably simply to have fun). Everyone recognizes that simply having fun must eventually give way to working for an end result, but when did that change for seven- and eight-year-olds?

There are many anecdotal examples of parents who have simply gone too far. Previous books have provided a litany of highly publicized events in which parents have made the news for their extreme actions, up to and including actually physically assaulting one another or, in rare cases, even killing each other. Bigelow et al. (2001) devoted an entire section of their book to the highlighting and discussion of specific assaults. The very fact that sections of books can be devoted to assaults involving parents at youth athletic events speaks for itself. During our research for this book, we came across a "hockey dad" (less famous, no doubt, than Sarah Palin's "hockey mom") who was so upset at his son's performance in a game, that he literally was yelling at the son in the backseat for what the father perceived as a lack of caring about the game and a lack of taking the game seriously. When met with his son's continued apathy about his own performance, the father stopped the car on a bridge and threw hundreds of dollars of hockey equipment into the river below. A point was surely made, but what really was the point? Was it that the son didn't take hockey as seriously as the father? That point was clearly made. Was it that the son should take hockey as seriously as the father, so that losing or performing poorly should become so consuming? That point is more tenuous.

One of the authors has been personally involved in the Little League draft—a draft taken so seriously by the coaches that many show up literally with their own binders of scouting reports about nine- and ten-year-old children they've seen play the year before in the "minor leagues." Long before Mitt Romney suggested that he had "binders full of women," Little League coaches across America had binders filled with the stats and profiles of nine- and ten-year-olds. Mitchell (2000) set the scene as follows: "As one kid followed another, the coaches stood along the foul line or sat in the dugout scribbling on pads like livestock judges" (21). Our own experiences parallel that description, with the exception of the setting, for given the New England weather, our tryouts were held in the middle school gym with rubber balls in the place of real baseballs so that no damage would be caused to the facility. Still, the scene and the characters seem interchangeable.

How strong was the child's arm? Could he or she hit? Hit for power? Run? Catch? Maybe those things seem obvious and are not necessarily symptomatic of the decline of our society. After all, shouldn't the fact that coaches would seek scouting reports about children's athletic ability merely be the due diligence required of a good and prepared coach? Winning is more fun than losing, after all, and almost everyone who has played organized sports would probably accept that adage. But for whom is winning more important? Is it as important for the children as it is for the coaches? Our experiences would suggest that in many cases, the emphasis upon winning comes far more from the coaches and parents than it does from the players, particularly when the players are young and just forming their own opinions about the sport in which they are involved.

While it may not be particularly important to the children to win a championship, it seems vital to the coaches (usually parents who have volunteered to coach) who make sure the draft follows more due process and involves more security than many defendants are afforded in our system of criminal justice. What is the strategy implemented to create the best draft class? Do you draft the best ten-year-old pitcher available? What if the best pitcher can't hit, but the second-best pitcher is a great hitter? What about the player's parents? Does the kid take vacations? Will he or she be committed to the proper degree? What if, and this is the ultimate horror, they play another sport that might take them away on a given Saturday or Saturdays? Are they then worth the risk of a high draft choice? (When one of the authors was engaging in this experience, one young man's father had made it known that his son could pitch, but only a little bit and only every third game, as he needed to save his arm for his Amateur Athletic Union [AAU] team.) It's not rocket science, but many would seemingly like it to be.

While all of that is going on at the high end, there's the more sociologically telling aspect of the draft, and the part that makes even some of the most committed volunteer coaches cringe: the discussions that ensue with regard to those picked toward the end of the draft. What about those children who clearly aren't very good athletes? What about those children who aren't even that interested in playing, and everyone knows it? While it may not be as unethical as what happened at Enron or WorldCom, shouldn't it nevertheless make us reflect on where we've gone societally, as some children are selected because their parents will take them on vacation and because they may ultimately quit and thus not become a burden at the back of the batting order? Is the ultimate

Little League bench player the child who desperately wants to play but isn't good enough to make the team better, or the child who really doesn't care and thus whose minimal playing time won't cause hard feelings with the parents? Mitchell (2000) brought forth another possible reason for picking players: the marital status or outward appearance of the mother: "Picking players based on their mother's looks, or marital status, is a youth sports tradition, even though I've never met a Little League manager who isn't married" (21). That little question of marital fidelity and integrity aside for now, other issues would be raised in our drafts, just as they were in Mitchell's descriptions: "When a talented boy botched a couple of ground balls, my friend and fellow coach . . . said 'someone wants to pick him in the draft and asked him to miss a few on purpose so no one else would take him.' A joke. Or was it? Considerable intrigue surrounds Little League tryouts and drafts" (22).

This environment allows for many unseemly occurrences on the field, when the draft has been completed and the games begin. We have personally seen parents who sign their children up for the league "late" so that they can attempt to manipulate which team their child would join. Others seek to be "assistant coaches" so that their sons or daughters can join with a head coach they seek, even though they actually have no intention or no time commitment to actually do any assistant coaching.

We have seen numerous incidents at Amateur Athletic Union (AAU) basketball games or middle school athletic events in which parents verbally abuse not only the officials (officials are accustomed to that, and when kept within limits, it probably does little to no harm to an official's self-esteem), but also the student volunteer time-keepers and scoreboard operators, and even some players on opposing teams. One particularly memorable incident involved a mom who positioned herself in a folding chair underneath the basket and taunted the opposing players in a way that wasn't traditionally very "mom-like." Why is it that people might become so personally vested (invested?) in their children's games? Why would a mother who may, in other venues, be a personally reasonable individual, feel compelled or even emboldened to taunt teenage boys on the other team? From whom did she learn that questioning a young man's sexuality or his masculinity or his athletic abilities would be an appropriate way to spend a Saturday afternoon?

Similar occurrences have been documented at youth soccer games, in which the taunting of opposing players, while not the norm, is far from unprecedented. One father with whom we spoke was ordered to write a letter of apology to the league for his taunting of officials during his son's game. Perhaps reflective of where we are, his fellow parents were far from upset with him, and in fact lent him their support with comments like "You only did and said what all of us were thinking and what all of us wanted to do." In interviewing his peer parents, we found that ten of the fourteen with whom we spoke fully supported his behavior. If peer pressure remains at all influential among "grown-ups," then the pressure exerted upon this individual certainly wouldn't seem to diminish his zeal, as his outbursts were by and large supported by his peers, not condemned. Children are not always as tolerant or unaffected by the actions of the adults on the sidelines: one incident with which we are familiar involved a young man who asked his soccer coach if he could play on the other side of the field, so that he could be a bit more removed from his parents' constant yelling at him. One of us had a similar personal experience with a young woman field hockey player who also requested that her coach keep her away from her parents. In another example we were told of a lacrosse coach who needed coaches on both sidelines, not for the benefit of the players, but to walk back and forth keeping parents in check.

We are all familiar with our own anecdotal examples, as well as newsworthy situations, involving overzealous parents seemingly more interested in their own perceptions of sports and their children's involvement in a way that may overshadow what their children themselves actually want from their games. But our emphasis upon these parents, who we suggest are perhaps overinvolved, isn't intended to overlook another opposite approach to parental involvement in youth sports: namely a lack of involvement. In our conversations with one another and our experiences interviewing parents, there are also many instances in which parents choose not to involve their children in organized sports. Choices that are made for our children, of course, lie fully within the proper discretion of parenting. Yet, in some cases, parents seem to deny the weight of those decisions and how those decisions affect their children and their children's involvement or lack of involvement in sports and other organized activities. Many parents choose not to enroll their children in their local sports leagues for a variety of reasons, and it would be folly to judge those decisions through only one lens. But what we can address is the reality that deciding not to enroll children in sports at a young age is every bit as conscious a parenting choice as is enrolling children in sports. The notion that young children make their own choices may be in larger part rationalization on the part of parents than it is a part of reality. It is easy to criticize the hyperinvolved parent who berates the officials at his or her child's soccer game, but we should also consider those children who aren't playing organized sports. Berating children at a sporting event is different in kind than not attending a sporting event at all, and the former quite clearly involves active harm above the latter.

Obviously, not every child is enrolled in organized youth sports, and thus it is impossible to assess any damage that might be done or that might mitigate the positive influences that sports may have on youth in every instance. But that recognition is important: just as children are subject to the "hyperinvolvement" of their parents, they just as surely are subject to choices made by their parents to keep their children away from organized sports. We all tend to rationalize our behaviors, regardless of our age, and our influences upon others in our lives. Our values are likewise represented by how we choose to spend our time and our money. Do we envy the member of the private country club? Or do we judge them as someone with either too much money or time on their hands? Do we question the money others spend on pursuits like golf, or objects like fancy cars, just as we might spend our own money on pursuits that others would find questionable? To some degree, of course we do. If we love golf or skiing or sailing, we often spend a lot of money on those pursuits, money that could clearly be spent on some more-worthwhile pursuit. Do we similarly judge those who love reading or marathon running or gambling? Our point is that we tend to involve ourselves in activities that we enjoy, and we justify our spending on these pursuits in ways that make sense to us but might be questioned by others.

It is easy to judge parents who enroll their children in youth sports and suggest that the emphasis they place upon sports may, in some instances, be too great, but what about those parents who are under the radar because they simply do not enroll their children in youth sports? We all understand how relatively easy it is to enroll your child in Little League or some other organized activity if the child comes to us and asks to be enrolled. Many of us had children ourselves or know of instances in which three-, four-, and five-year-olds come to their parents and ask to be involved in a given sport or activity. But what about children who don't ask? Have they really made a mature decision not to be involved in sports? We know of parents who don't enroll their children in Little League, not because they are opposed to their children playing softball or baseball, but because they themselves don't want to give up their Saturdays taxiing their children to practice or altering family plans because children will need to attend practice and games.

A parent from a rural part of Minnesota remembers her childhood being much more laid back. She acknowledges it could be regional, as they live in a rural part of the state and enjoy being in an environment like that, but says the kids today "committed to a sport are dedicated to it almost like they are going to be Olympians. It's like, that is it. You're not going camping, you're not doing this or that, you're just committed to the sport." But for her what is ironic is that they say the most important thing is family, but the family is spending all the time at games and traveling to games. In her family they are committed to camping, especially in the summertime, and there was no way they wanted to be traveling. She wants her sons to have different experiences and not just to be able to experience one thing—sports. As a parent she believes she made a conscious effort not to force them into sports. And as she states, "Even if you wanted to put as much as you can in, there's other things you need to do. We had other things that didn't have to do with the sport but we had practice every night so it just did not work."

Time commitments to sports usually involve much more now than simply giving up a Saturday morning, and some parents are quite aware that what might simply start with Saturday morning soccer at a very young age may easily progress into organized activities nearly every night of the week. One of our interview subjects, who we will call Christine, lives in a suburb of Columbus, Ohio, and is a forty-five-year-old mother of three. Her children, at the time of the interview, were ten, eight, and preschool age. Her quote below discusses the time commitment her family sets aside in the summer for sports:

> Sports-wise both older kids play travel baseball so that takes up time from the 1st of June until the middle of July. Between the two of them, it's actually slowed down a little bit, from what its peak was, but we could have games maybe four or five times a week during that

time. They have football practice all summer, or conditioning for high school. So that's four days a week all summer long until two-a-days start and that's every day for two and a half weeks or whatever. So that's pretty much all summer. We try to take a week's vacation. Sometimes it's related to a baseball tournament. Two years ago we went to Disney World for a tournament so it was kind of a combination vacation and tournament. We've been to nationals and stuff like that. So it really revolves around baseball season. And as soon as that's done football season starts.

This family illustrates the importance that sports plays in the "nonsports" lives of a family, as even summer family "vacations" become centered around the child's or children's sporting lives. The notion of taking the family on a cross-country trip to the National Parks, whether glamourized from our youth or satirized by the Griswolds of the National Lampoon Vacation movies, is becoming another distant memory, as parents no longer control the agenda; in many cases, the activities of the child control the agenda.

The method of avoiding that potential commitment by not allowing a child to involve themselves in organized sports is a very real phenomenon in our society. While it is not our intent to indict such decision making, it nevertheless must be acknowledged that such decision making has a very real effect upon a child's future involvement in sports and may affect the child's general attitude toward organized sports as they develop and mature. Perhaps using the analogy of religion is appropriate (particularly given the religious fervor that accompanies some of our devotion to sports). Many parents force their young children to participate in religious activities at a young age; it's not as if very small children typically make a request to begin attending religious services. Parents often suggest that by requiring their children to involve themselves in the parents' religious beliefs, that they are merely instilling in their children the ability to ultimately choose for themselves how involved they may be in religion. Such a belief that taking one's young child to religious training allows that child freedom to choose more wisely later in life, is, of course, perfectly valid; nevertheless, it is indeed a belief. It is impossible to predict with any real certainty whether that religious training will better inform a given child, or whether it will instead indoctrinate that child into accepting the parents' beliefs.

It would be disingenuous, we think, for parents to suggest that three-, four-, or five-year olds should always be allowed to make those choices for themselves, just as it seems inappropriate for three-, four-, or five-year-olds to be burdened with the decision to participate in sports or other organized activities. Forced participation in sports is obviously a very negative thing, and many of our anecdotes suggest the damage caused by parents who make their children participate in things that seem more for the benefit of the parent than in accord with the interests of the child. But likewise "forced nonparticipation" might be equally damaging.

Many young people grow up hating sports or otherwise feeling antipathy toward those who participate largely because of the socialization they've undergone at home, similar to the socialization they've undergone with regard to either actively participating in religion or not. Does a parent's attitude that might negatively socialize a child toward involvement in sports correlate to physical inactivity later in life? Parents who portray sports as negative, and thus don't allow their children to participate, are perhaps doing their children a disservice just as much as the more-traditional overzealous helicopter parents who involve themselves too much. While it may not be equal in kind to expose one's child to parents who berate officials and otherwise involve themselves inappropriately in uncivil behavior, it still may nevertheless be potentially harmful to prevent children from engaging in youth sports because of the discretion and the convenience choices made by parents.

Perhaps any discussion of religion should properly end with an admonition against judging parental decision making too harshly, whether those decisions involve engaging their children in organized sports or avoiding organized sports. The notion that any generalization can be made about which is ultimately better for each child is pure folly; our point is simply to suggest that parents make decisions for their children, and deciding *not* to involve one's child in organized sports is often no less selfish than the decision made to involve a child in organized sports. The problem presented as parents attempt to live vicariously through their children happens not only in the world of sports, but it would seem that many parents, if not most parents, tend to parent their children in the manner that they believe best serves their children (and themselves); sometimes that means involvement in youth sports, sometimes it doesn't, but both are very conscious decisions made that have a lasting impact, for better and for worse, upon children.

It seems intellectually dishonest to expect children to not conform to the socialization they receive at home. Young children who carry signs in parades protesting major social causes have likely not come to these beliefs on their own and have not formed these conclusions without serious influence. Many of us cringe when we see young children carrying signs against or in support of major social causes that involve complicated issues clearly beyond the realm of the child's understanding. Involving that child in the parents' cause is certainly a form of parental influence that far exceeds any pretense that the child is making their own decisions. Is the five-year-old who tries a sport because her parents make her try the sport any more damaged than the five-year-old who attends religious services because her parents make her try religion? Is making a child try a sport, or for that matter is making a child take piano lessons, things that the child will ultimately be free to pursue or reject, any different in kind from making them try a food they may later embrace or reject, but will surely never try on their own?

Tiger Woods was forced to "like" playing golf (and many are familiar with the iconic picture of the toddler Tiger illustrating his golfing prowess on the old Mike Douglas show at the age of two). Tiger's appearance, including an iconic photograph of him alongside Mike Douglas, Earl Woods, Bob Hope, and Jimmy Stewart, is well chronicled in *The Passion of Tiger Woods* (2011) written by the anthropologist Orin Starn. Obviously, Tiger serves as a vivid example of a person being truly groomed to succeed in a given sport, and his success in that sport surely validates his father's ability to recognize potential.

Tiger, of course, while an exceptional story, is not entirely unique. Venus and Serena Williams were forced to "like" playing tennis; Yo-Yo Ma was forced to "like" making music. If their parents had never forced them to do these things, would they have been happier? Would they have been more successful? It is difficult to imagine any of them being more successful at another endeavor than they are at their "chosen" professions . . . but did they really "choose"? If parents aren't allowed to put a tennis racket or a golf club or a musical instrument in a child's hands, and instead we encourage children only to make their "own choices," then how different the world would be. Perhaps even more interesting, how different and diminished would many various professions clearly be, as those listed above are but a few examples of those who began their pursuits at extremely early ages and managed to rise to the top of their respective games?

Our local newspaper, the *Providence Journal*, on Sunday, July 14, 2013, featured articles in the sports page about two standout athletes: Martina Hingis's induction into the Tennis Hall of Fame and Rob Gronkowski (professional football) discussing his father's book, *Growing up Gronk* (2013). Reading these articles would seem to validate hyperinvolvement of parents in their children's sporting development. Martina Hingis's mother put a tennis racquet in her daughter's hand at the age of two and she was competing by the time she was four (Szostak 2013, C5). Rob Gronkowski's father put a gym in their family's basement so his five sons could become better athletes, telling his sons "if they wanted to take it to the next level, they needed to keep ahead of everyone else" (Reynolds 2013, C7). The fact that "success" stories like these, and the attention they receive in the media, sometimes encourage overeager parents to begin pushing their children at an amazingly early age is almost indisputable.

Time magazine's July 22, 2013, issue featured an article entitled "Final Four for the 4-Foot Set," which chronicled some of the issues facing the second-grade national basketball champions. "Each coach wrestles with how to handle the hotel pool. The kids want to jump in— 'Cannonball'—but all that splashing around can leave them sluggish on the court. On the other hand, tiring the players out a bit helps them fall asleep earlier, which can keep them fresh for game time" (Gregory 2013, 46). Is that anecdote humorous . . . or sad? Another fine line we guess. What it does point out is another example of the societal obsession with success at an early age and the power of organized sports in our lives.

These examples are obviously somewhat extreme. Most parents who encourage or even force their children to play a given sport at a young age are not creating a professional athlete. In some cases, they may not even be creating an athlete at all. Still, it would seem that again there remains a difficult and fine line between useful encouragement and obsessive demands.

The perception that young people themselves want to become professional athletes is often true. In the past surely it was as common for a young boy to want to grow up to play major league baseball as it was for him to want to be a fireman or a cowboy. As that young boy aged, he likely began to form different interests and perhaps a different and more realistic view of his future life in which professional baseball would not be a likely outcome. Today, many girls have similar "major league dreams" through the development of the Women's National Basketball Association (WNBA) and the National Women's Soccer League (NWSL) for example. We found it in our interviews too. Grant, a fourteen-year-old eighth grader, lives in an Ohio suburb. He presented himself as a stereotypical teenager, right down to the adolescent acne and his fit and trim athletic look. You could see that his face was changing during adolescence. Grant was asked why he was so interested in sports and recreation. His answer suggested that he quite clearly saw himself as an athlete.

> Well, I'd say I'm gifted athletically so I use my ability and play sports. And it keeps me in shape. And it is fun and time consuming so I like it. My dad was really athletic and my mom was athletic and I have potential in being good in sports so I can just do stuff that some people can't do because they weren't born with it. I want to get a scholarship in a sport and go there [college] and maybe just try to walk on and play a pro sport.

Ultimately, as children age and mature they will come to decisions on their own, and they may embrace or reject sports just as they may embrace or reject religion as that religion serves their needs; but to suggest that children who aren't encouraged to play sports at an early age have already chosen to reject organized sports is disingenuous at best. The decision was made for them; we hope it was made with their consent, but whether it was made with real coercion or more subtle coercion, it was nevertheless a decision made for the child, by the parent or parents.

Parents find themselves in a bit of a quandary: encouraging a child's dreams, even if those dreams seem unrealistic, has always been perceived to be the role of a parent. Isn't it simply good parenting to encourage one's son or daughter to follow their dreams of one day playing in the NBA or WNBA, even if the child is on the small side? If the answer is yes, then nevertheless, there must come a time when the parent must help the child assess his or her reality and thus begin to shape a positive future. In other words, just as we must encourage our children to follow their dreams, we must also guard against false and unrealistic expectations. In the world of sports, we have come to know that certain truisms exist: large people cannot become jockeys or coxswains on the crew team or gymnasts. The market simply won't allow for it. Raising this awareness in our children, even if it means ending their pursuit of unrealistic goals, seems to lie somewhere on the spectrum between being entirely helpful and being entirely mean-spirited. The difficulty of parenting, and parenting well, rears its ugly head yet again. Zerubavel (2006) wrote eloquently of the "elephant in the room" in his book of the same name. Many of our conversations with children about their sporting futures have the potential of missing the "elephant in the room." Ignoring through silence what should sometimes be obvious may not be the preferred manner of handling difficult decisions, but nevertheless it is an extremely common response, and parenting is no different: we sometimes choose to ignore the elephant in the room and do our best to muddle through in silence or complete denial. Sometimes that denial seems obvious to those outside of the situation. We have all been witness and subjected to parents who have unrealistic perceptions of their children's abilities. Or at least their perceptions seem unrealistic to us. To us, in fact, it sometimes seems like they are simply ignoring the elephant in the room. Their child is simply aging out of a given sport; they are clearly too small or too large for future success; or they are clearly not as talented as their peers and opponents, so future dreams should obviously be tempered. But the "obviousness" is apparent only to those on the outside, not so much to those on the inside of the situation.

HELICOPTER PARENTS

Many of the scenarios we've described in this chapter involve instances of helicopter parenting—parents who almost literally hover above their children as a helicopter hovers above traffic seeing all and reporting to us about what is taking place below. Parents often hover over their children's activities to such an extent that when something happens, there is no time for the child to make his or her own decision about how best to deal with it, as the parent has already swooped in to save the day. Obviously, generalizations are difficult, and the concept of hovering over one's child, in today's environment, is somewhat different than what it once would have been. Children are sometimes endangered in today's world. Many of the dangers we see lurking are indeed real, but still others are simply perceptions that may not be based in reality. The thought of merely sending a young child down the street to the play-ground on his or her own might be even more potentially dangerous to the child's health than hovering over them at all times.

Parents are as different as children are different, and parenting styles come in a variety of shapes and sizes. An example of these differences is seen when a young athlete is injured in competition. Many parents arrive upon the scene in the middle of the action almost before the referee blows his or her whistle to stop play. Other parents, no less concerned, remain on the sidelines until or unless summoned by the coach or trainer. One must imagine that many children have later confronted their parents about such parental choices, and while some children may lament parents who seem too cavalier about injuries suffered, many others express differing levels of embarrassment concerning parents who are too quick to intervene no matter what the situation. It is difficult to condemn the conduct of a concerned parent who rushes out onto the playing field when it is clear that his or her son or daughter has been injured; after all, most of us aren't at our best when faced with crisis situations. Still, it would seem that expressing appropriate concern is different from engaging in conduct unbecoming a spectator at a sporting event, even if that spectator is a parent.

As with many children's activities, many of the problems we can properly attribute to Little League and other organized sports for children seem to stem from the conduct of the parents rather than the participants themselves. When we consider the ills of youth sports, we usually lament parents who berate officials and their own and other children and coaches who seemingly act as though the games were more important for their own edification than for the development of the children involved. While coaches suffer untold criticisms, many justified, it remains true that among thankless jobs in our society, coaching children's teams must surely rank near the top. Parents demand playing time for their children, often myopically viewing the team through only the lens of one player (their son or daughter). While most of us don't enjoy others outside our fields of expertise telling us how to do our jobs, coaches must endure a steady onslaught of such "advice."

Just as helicopter parents hover over their children, many parents hover over coaches and allow them little freedom to exercise their discretion. Nearly all of the coaches we've spoken with regarding youth sports have suggested the reason they ultimately quit coaching, or at least frequently consider quitting, is not because of the players, but because of the parents.

When sports become a ticket (real or more often perceived) to opportunities such as higher education and maybe even an express route to the majors, the atmosphere has changed. No longer can Johnny or Jane try baseball at the age of nine or ten for the sake of trying a new sport, because their peers have been in training since age five in order to be competitive. Coaches often do not want to "deal with the new kids" as they focus their energy on their budding superstars who have "chosen" their sports before they were old enough to choose their own bedtime. Children are being pressured into specializing on a sport so that they can achieve greatness when they are at an age in which their career aspirations are sometimes entirely disconnected from reality.

The ability of parents to mask their own behavior and act in a way that would be viewed as objectively inappropriate if it were done in the workplace, at home, or in some public venue, may be deemed perfectly acceptable, if not mainstream, when engaged upon at a Little League field. In other words, parents cannot scream and chastise their bosses or coworkers, their spouses or children, but it has become somewhat commonplace to denigrate coaches, players on opposing teams, and most assuredly, the umpires/referees. Persons who are deemed reasonable and responsible citizens have a certain freedom from the social controls that compel civil behavior in the workplace and elsewhere, as they may lash out with impunity at a Little League game. Bill Geist (1992) humorously includes the following quote in his book *Little League Confidential*, which he attributes to the mother of one of his players: "I tell my shrink I'm like Jekyll and Hyde. . . . I turn into a monster at Little League games, and I can't stop myself" (8). In defense of that mother, the more games a parent attends, the more educated one becomes and the more able one becomes to distinguish between good and competent refereeing and that which seems decidedly less good and competent. This, of course, comes with the necessary caveat suggesting that recognizing good refereeing doesn't mean agreeing with every call a referee makes, nor does it suggest that a good referee is one that favors the team with which the spectator in question has a rooting interest. It would seem that at some level parents find a certain freedom in using their power as spectators to berate those they deem worthy of their wrath. Perhaps because they cannot act this way in their "real lives," it seems empowering to act this way in their kids' sporting lives.

The irony, perhaps, lies not only on the children who are compelled to determine their life course while they believe in Santa Claus and the Tooth Fairy, but also upon the parents who believe Santa will actually deliver to them a major leaguer or at least a collegiate scholarship. The idea that all children will simply be able to enjoy playing the game of baseball may now be in the past, given the pressures exerted upon them, having gone by the wayside just like the idea of being able to afford to take the family to Fenway Park, Yankee Stadium, or most other major league stadiums. The ultimate goal of this chapter is to foster increased discussion of whether or not children's sports programs are in danger of having their worthwhile objectives of fostering character development, teamwork, discipline, and so forth, perverted into an environment in which what is actually learned is the importance of parental influence and incivility. We hope that by using Little League baseball as a lens through which we view parental influence and behavior that we contribute to the larger discussion of increased incivility in our society and the role of sports in American culture.

Still, we love sports. Despite all that can go wrong, despite all that does go wrong, and despite our knowledge that much harm can be done and often is done, we nevertheless love sports. While addiction may be too strong a word, and isn't meant to convey a diminishment of the understanding of those who suffer from more traditionally considered addictions, it would seem as though sports, for many of us, is a real addiction. We cannot get enough, even when we know we've had too much. Perhaps, for us at least, it's merely a healthy obsession. There is a fine line between one person's addiction and another's healthy obsession.

WORKS CITED

Associated Press. "When Parents Hover over Kids' Job," msnbc.com, last modified November 7, 2006. http://www.studyplace.org/w/images/3/39/Parents_hover.pdf.

Bigelow, Bob, Tom Moroney, and Linda Hall. *Just Let the Kids Play: How to Stop Other Adults from Ruining Your Child's Fun and Success in Youth Sports*. Deerfield Beach, FL: Health Communications, Inc., 2001.

Fortin, Judy. "Hovering Parents Need to Step Back at College Time." *Health Minute*, February 4, 2008. http://www.cnn.com/2008/HEALTH/family/02/04/hm.helicopter.parents/.

Geist, Bill. *Little League Confidential: One Coach's Completely Unauthorized Tale of Survival*. New York: Macmillan Publishing Company, 1992.

Gregory, Sean. "Final Four for the 4-Foot Set." *Time* Magazine, July 2013: 44–48.

Gronkowski, Gordon. *Growing up Gronk: A Family's Story of Raising Champions*. Boston: Houghton-Mifflin, 2013.

Jayson, Sharon. "Helicopter Parents Cross All Ages, Social Lines. " usatoday.com, April 3, 2007. http://usatoday30.usatoday.com/news/nation/2007-04-03-helicopter-study_n.htm.

Mitchell, Greg. *Joy in Mudville: A Little League Memoir*. New York: Washington Square Press, 2000.

Reynolds, Bill. "Gronk's Dad Ingrained Fierce Work Ethic in Sons." *Providence Journal*, July 14, 2013: C7.

Starn, Orin. *The Passion of Tiger Woods: An Anthropologist Reports on Golf, Race, and Celebrity Scandal*. Durham, NC: Duke University Press, 2011.

Szostak, Mike. "Hingis Among Inductees." *Providence Journal*, July 14, 2013: C, C5.

Zerubavel, Eviatar. *The Elephant in the Room: Silence and Denial in Everyday Life*. New York: Oxford University Press, 2006.

3

"ATHLETIC CAPITAL"

Status, Performance, and Physical Activity Level among Middle School Students

Why do certain young people see themselves as athletes or nonathletes? Is it because of a variety of differences among and between the perceptions that people have of themselves and their own athletic abilities and interests, as well as their perceptions of how others see them? Some characteristics that we all have seem self-evident: are we short or are we tall? Most adults probably look at ourselves in a mirror and have long accepted (even if we aren't comfortable with our appearance) our lot in life when it comes to how tall or short we may be. No doubt some of us wish we were taller, others wish they were shorter, and maybe (hopefully) most of us are content with what we see. As adults, we've likely "accepted" our individual lots in life, at least with regard to what we can change and what we cannot. But children, and teenagers in particular, are often uncomfortable with what they see in the mirror. Most teenagers have a certain level of discomfort with what they see reflected back at them. Almost any person who has had a serious conversation with a teenager, from a parent to a teacher, coach, or counselor, can easily relate to the gulf between how most teenagers wished they looked and how they believe that they appear to others. Aside even from the all-too-common teenage trauma of acne and braces and other indignities, there was perhaps the simplest overgeneralization of all: most of us remember the teenage years in which males almost universally wanted to be bigger and females almost universally wished they were smaller.

Perhaps it may even be a possibility that words like tall and short are inherently subjective: "I may be short by most people's standards, but I'm tall for my family" or "I may be tall for a hockey player, but I'm short for a basketball player." But what about characteristics that are even more subjective and not immediately apparent to outside observers? "I am athletic" or "I am uncoordinated and couldn't possibly do athletic things." Anyone who has ever played a game of pickup basketball with strangers knows how wrong we can be about our perceptions of others, as we've all seen instances in which a player is "much better than he or she looks" or in some cases "isn't as athletic as he or she looked." Maybe some are familiar with the Tyree Irving YouTube video in which he used makeup to portray himself as a much older and nonathletic-looking man, rather than his real persona as a National Basketball Association (NBA) star for the Cleveland Cavaliers. In the video, the young men playing pickup basketball are forced to allow Tyree to play after one of the ten goes down with an injury. Reluctantly, they allow him entry and lament his seeming inability to play at their level. But then, as if by magic, Tyree transforms into the real Tyree and begins dominating the play and boggling the minds of those who perceived him to be something entirely different. While that video was made in good humor, it nevertheless proves the point that looks can indeed be deceiving in the world of athletic ability.

What do these subjective measures based on physical appearance really mean, and of particular importance: what do these measures really mean for young people who are just coming to terms with their changing bodies, their changing levels of coordination and comfort with those bodies, and their even more general awkwardness that accompanies one's coming of age? As a teenager the thought of being judged by one's appearance can be a truly frightening prospect. The relatively short basketball players or the small football players must first overcome the judgments of others even before they consider playing the game, and if they overcome that first obstacle and decide to play the game, then they will be judged even before they enter the game. Only after they enter the game might they be judged upon their abilities. While an NBA player might be comfortable with being picked last because he knows when he enters the game that he'll be able to change people's perceptions in a hurry, it's not so easy for others who fear not only being picked last in the pickup game, but being chastised for their athletic performance once they enter the fray. While the chastisement from coaches (implicit and explicit) is damaging enough, potential chastisement from peers is an even greater concern. "Making and keeping friends is a major focus for children ages 6-12, as significant as school and certainly more important than the number of sports trophies they may win" (Ginsburg et al. 2006, 53).

Addressing the issues of self-esteem that accompany being picked last is a fear that many parents have for their children and a reality for many others. Welch (1995) addressed this in a children's book, *Playing Right Field*, in which the young boy learns the value of his contributions to the team, even though he begins with the painful realization that he is always picked last and is always relegated to right field. Right field, of course, is that place where dreams go to die in Little League, as even novice baseball and softball players recognize that location as the place where traditionally the weakest players are positioned. (For a variety of reasons, as one ages through Little League and into high school and beyond, right field is no longer considered the "weakest" outfield position, but there is little dispute that it has traditionally been considered the place to hide less-skilled players at an early age.) Sports are no different from other avenues in life in which the difficulty of overcoming stereotyping and the perceptions of others is no small feat. Much has been written about the wage gap and other gender-related issues in which women have long suffered societal judgments concerning their relative worth in the marketplace and the business world. Overcoming these gaps takes time, patience, and an ability to endure consistent levels of frustration. Similarly, overcoming the perceptions of others regarding one's athletic ability can be equally frustrating, if the initial stereotyping means that someone else (a coach, a parent) has used his or her judgment in a way that creates another obstacle for some that others don't face. We wrote earlier of the phenomenon in which the coach's son gets to be the quarterback, in some cases almost by default. The advantages that ensue from that are, in many ways, self-evident. But the opposite story is no less real: the young person whose outward appearance seems to assure their placement in "right field," which makes their development in sports more difficult. Being labeled as the right-fielder can be every bit as persistent as being labeled the short-stop.

While we have played on athletic teams from elementary school through college, we also have a number of friends who see themselves as nonathletes. What determines the way in which a person sees him- or herself? Why do some young people move forward athletically, while others lag behind, and still others abandon any pretense of athletic involvement? How does the *athletic capital* of some middle school students affect the physical activity level of students in this age group? Students who have "athletic skills"—what we will call "athletic capital"—enjoy a special status in the classroom, among their peers, and within the larger community. While the term athletic capital may be relatively new, most of us are familiar with the concept of social capital, and of capital more broadly. President George W. Bush once famously said that he had *political capital* after his reelection, and he intended to "spend it" (Stevenson 2004).

So while we are all familiar with how we might spend our own social capital, or how politicians might spend their (real or perceived) political capital, we are focused upon how young people are able to parlay their athletic capital into similar accrued benefits, or how those who lack athletic capital cannot leverage it. Like the other forms of capital, in which those who have it can spend it, and those who don't can only watch others spend it, this type of capital similarly creates a system of stratification among young people based on their physical activities. While we may not be entirely comfortable with the reality of economic class divisions in our society, to suggest that they don't exist would be folly. Likewise, athletic capital creates significant and meaningful divisions in our society, especially among the youth—the division between those who possess athletic capital and thus spend it on the athletic fields and gym classes, and those who don't possess much athletic capital and are resigned to watch others spend what they themselves simply don't have.

For the purposes of our discussion we are defining middle school–age children as students in public school grades six, seven, eight, and in some cases nine. We acknowledge that there are vast differences within this group in terms of physical development and perception. For example, one sixth-grade girl in Nebraska who was interviewed about cliques or groups in her school thought about it a bit before answering and then said the only group she could think of that she belonged to was the blue bird reading group—she was not yet aware or able to verbalize cliques in her experience. But the seventh-, eighth-, and ninth-grade students who were interviewed, perhaps not surprisingly, could pretty readily identify cliques in which they were personally involved and, sometimes painfully, cliques in which they clearly were not.

If you take a moment to think back to middle school, you can probably remember quite a few separate cliques—some had hard and fast boundaries; others were less defined. Many middle schoolers we spoke to felt as though they are fully entrenched in some groups, for better and worse, and others felt as if they are "in" one moment and "out" the next. The cliques of our own youths remain present today. There may be more variations than any of us may remember but they are still there. Maybe even the way we refer to cliques has changed, but that hasn't necessarily lessened their presence. Social media seems to exacerbate the awareness of certain cliques and the divides among students.

After taking that moment to remember middle school cliques, take another moment to remember your physical education classes (gym classes). Some of you may have been active participants, while others were always looking for a way to get out of gym class. Most of us perhaps fell somewhere between those two extremes, perhaps based on the activity of the day. We liked playing basketball or softball, for example, but weren't too enamored with physical agility drills. But all of us can probably remember at least one or two people who were very good at the physical education activities and were praised for those skills by the teachers and their peers. You may also remember the students who were not good at the required physical education activities and who sometimes consequently may have taken pains to avoid gym class. The fact that such occurrences still reign supreme in middle schools across the country would probably not surprise anyone, and our observations of physical education (PE) classes, middle school cocurricular activities, cafeterias, and libraries, and interviews with students themselves, confirmed that there is still a special status awarded to students who are good in PE. Those with certain skills are considered natural athletes even as young as middle school. If special and elite status is somehow bestowed upon those who are good at gym class, it quite naturally follows that lesser status accompanies those who struggle.

A corollary perhaps can be found in all classes in schools: after all, math class is likely populated with those who function at a high level, those who struggle mightily, and most who fall somewhere in between. One potential difference lies in the fact that in the academic areas, there are options in which the best students can and do take the more difficult classes, and those who struggle can be in class with others in similar circumstances; that's not typically the case in physical education.

It should probably not surprise us when young people who struggle in school choose unfortunate alternatives like dropping out, or the less-radical approach of denying the value of courses in which they have little success. Many reading these words right now (and maybe even the authors of these words) may have been guilty themselves of rationalizing their own lack of math skills as somehow unimportant to their larger lives. Sometimes people generally may have even suggested that those who were good at math were "geeks" or in some other way less appealing than the rest of us who weren't so good at math. Those who struggle with their physical skills aren't so very different in kind from those of us who struggle with our math skills, and sometimes similarly suggest that those who don't struggle in that department are "dumb jocks" or otherwise less appealing than themselves. The power of rationalization seems paramount regardless of what skills or lack of skills might be justified. Still, it would seem, particularly in the teenage years, that the stigma that is potentially associated with being nonathletic is far greater, and therefore potentially far more damaging emotionally, than any such stigma attached to being bad at math or other academic pursuits. All of us are quite capable of rationalizing our own beliefs and behaviors; certainly we learn those rationalization skills in middle school or even before. As adults we even laud these skills as "coping" mechanisms. The fine line between appropriate coping and less-appropriate rationalizing appears razor thin.

Students' physical capabilities, including their coordination and athletic skills as middle school students, affect their perceptions of self as they grow older. The students that were interviewed for this book wanted to talk about how they saw each other—that was important to them. The cliques were part of their everyday life. They were asked about what they did outside of school, family life, and academic subjects, but it was the social experience of school that they wanted to share: how they saw the culture of their schools and how their peers acted in their groups. Students could see how groups were created and what type of status and power a group had. These young students are creating and recognizing their identities in relation to each other and their peer groups, school, family, and other social institutions, but what we think may be overlooked is the part of their identity that is forming in relation to physical movement. And it is that relationship that gives a person athletic capital. Athletic capital increases status in the "jock" clique, which is associated with being cool and well-liked and is one of the highest forms of popularity among peers. Our interviews with middle school youth, as well as our discussions with parents and our own personal experiences, suggest that the level of disdain that some hold for the "jocks" is further evidence of the power that such status carries.

In Eckert's *Jocks and Burnouts: Social Categories and Identity in the High School* (1989), she discusses the polar opposite nature of the two groups. Eckert suggested that the jocks buy into the school paradigms, while the burnouts . . . not so much. Schools obviously are designed to reward those who buy into their own created paradigms and structures, and thus it should be of no surprise that schools tend to reward student-athletes and those athletes tend to buy into the culture of the education system (even if some of them individually don't always buy into the value of education itself). Schools tend to prominently feature trophy cases honoring athletic accomplishment; but it would be difficult to find an area lauding "burnouts" who by definition have "burned out" of the system and have not fully or sometimes even partially bought into the culture of the educational system of which they are a part. Put most simply, some students have built up athletic capital that they are free to spend with their peers and even with some of their teachers, in order to make their lives better (just like the economic capital we acquire in our capitalist system). It would be absurd to suggest that the rich don't have the power to acquire things to make their lives better, and it would be equally nonsensical to assert that some students with capital don't have a similar power to make their situations better as well. Some students acquire social capital—they are popular for a variety of reasons—perhaps because of their physical attractiveness, their ability to amuse others, their friendly natures, or their intellectual prowess. Just as some acquire social capital and spend it freely, others may acquire athletic capital and use it every bit as effectively to enrich their experiences in the hallways and in the classrooms, just as surely as they use it on the athletic fields.

We believe that there are two elements to the construction of athletic capital. The first is having fine and large motor skills, kinetic skills, coordination, speed, and stamina—whether that is natural physical coordination or what Western culture deems as the "right" coordination to participate in school-sanctioned physical activities and sports. Coordination translates quite simply into being good at a given activity and having the self-awareness and self-confidence that assure a person that he or she is indeed "good at something." Young athletes provide many examples of that self-awareness that suggest they recognize where their capital exists, and how they can properly use it. Henry, a thirteen-year-old eighth grader who lives in a Virginia suburb, illustrates this self-recognition. Henry tried lots of sports, but stuck with swimming simply because he believed he was just good at it. It wasn't seemingly as relevant if Henry "liked" swimming, or may have liked some other sport more; it simply was a matter of using his athletic capital in the most logical way: "I was swimming since I was young. Like I tried tennis and I did baseball for a year or two. I tried skiing. I did skiing [downhill] for a little bit. [Swimming stuck] because I realized that I was good at it."

A second part of athletic capital is whether there are the means and knowledge to invest in the child's potential athletic prowess. For example, does the family have the financial resources, time, motivation, interest, and desire to invest in their child's physical activity? It can be argued that each one of these pieces could be independent of each other, but in most cases they work together.

There are significant differences in physical growth during middle school. This is one of the reasons middle school can be so difficult: there is so much change in three years. Some people may naturally have fine and large motor skills, kinetic skills, coordination, speed, and stamina; others learn or grow into them as they age. However, how people play and participate in sport is culturally constructed. As Dyck and Archetti (2003) state: "These identities inevitably reflect not only stylized forms of movement and purpose, but also contexts within which they are nurtured" (1). A person's culture is embodied in his or her every action—from walking and dancing to playing a sport. While we can discuss socialization—how one becomes socialized in one's culture from elements such as etiquette, language, and style—embodiment goes further, into a total orientation of our being. Through culture people learn how to use their bodies in space, and to use large and fine motor skills to complete specific tasks. Examples of this are seen every day in physical education classes—children try to make their bodies work to perform the physical skills required to participate in the class activity exactly as the teacher asked. Again, think back to your middle school PE classes. The children who could dribble and shoot a basketball, kick a soccer ball, do push-ups and pull-ups, and run a mile in a certain time were all deemed to have the physical prowess to succeed in gym. The individuals who could not do some of these activities well were seen as unathletic and labeled nonathletes, even though this is a time of major physical development. This labeling could, and does, have long-term implications for how these young people see themselves and consequently how physically active they become.

The second area includes having the means and knowledge to invest in the child's body—financial resources and time to invest in the child's physical activity. Along with individual coordination, a child needs support to enhance his or her physical abilities and gain "athletic capital."

Participating in youth sports requires an investment of the family's resources (e.g., money and time). A good example is the Ohio mother of three who shared with us that her four-year-old was already prepping to follow his older brothers into athletics. In this short narrative she explains that being involved in sports at a young age is important to this family and that the parents' time, money, and interest in sports are paramount.

> My four-year-old preschooler does swimming lessons and is going to start ice skating lessons. He goes to the little gym. He's in a sports class so they do a little bit of gymnastics for the balance and stuff but they'll key on different sports. So they're doing basketball right now with the Little Tikes basketball thing. They've done soccer and they're going to do football. And he's taken some other little sport things at Sports Ohio. We have a lot of stuff in the area available. So he's done soccer and T-ball and stuff like that there.

She continues by talking about her husband's involvement in her two older sons' sports careers:

> My husband was the coach for football for both my older kids when they were doing the intramural stuff. And he coached them both in baseball too or has at various times. He coached them in soccer too actually.

These parents obviously place importance on having their children involved in organized sports. They had the finances to have their four-year-old participate in sport classes, and a parent was able to give his time to coaching his older two sons' sports teams. For most families, this means that a parent's past history and/or interest in sports is important. Just as those parents who value reading read to their children, or those who value religion involve their children in religious activities, those who tend to value sports tend to similarly influence and involve their children in sporting activities. When there is a history of sports participation with the parents, it allows for more opportunities for a child to participate.

EXAMINING ATHLETIC CAPITAL FOR MIDDLE SCHOOL–AGE CHILDREN

By developing and using athletic skills, students gain or reinforce athletic capital throughout their school career to gain status. The opposite is also true. If a child is lacking athletic skills, or believes he or she lacks athletic skills, this can reinforce nonparticipation and lower status. Without positive reinforcement, a child often will not want to continue working to develop athletic skills, especially if peers tease the child in gym class. As with many things, a self-fulfilling prophecy develops as a negatively reinforced person simply stops doing those things that result in negative reinforcement, and thus, logically, they have little hope at improving at the activity.

A closer examination of physical education classes offers insights into how athletic capital is gained and reinforced, and how an individual without natural or learned physical capabilities can be left behind. Harold is a small, kind of skinny kid, who, at the time of the interview, was an eleven-year-old sixth grader. He was very articulate and made the interview extremely enjoyable. He had just started sixth grade in a new building, and he was very open about how that new experience was somewhat nerve-racking for him. He was very open about being nervous and related how he was scared about figuring out how to open his locker: "I was really, really scared at first. I was so nervous that when I was opening my locker my hands were shaking." The interview then turned to physical education and sports:

> We're doing volleyball right now [in gym class]. And I like volleyball; I just don't really like this because we're not doing games and they didn't really teach us how to play. We just play a regular volleyball game but no one knows how to play. No one knows how to hit the ball and it's really annoying. It just goes over and hits the ground. I don't think that very many people like volleyball.

While we cannot determine what will become of Harold over the course of time, it seems likely that volleyball will not play much of a role in his future. Whether or not Harold grows into a more self-assured, confident young man, and whether or not he pursues athletics in any real way, it is clear that a lack of confidence goes some distance toward eliminating a desire to pursue a given subject. Stories like these suggest that the reinforcement that young people receive in athletics, and in gym class, shapes their development not just as athletes but, more importantly, as participants. Not having seen the gym class to which Harold referred, we are reluctant to blame the teacher for Harold's loss of interest in the activity. In fact, just as we college professors sometimes lament the difficulty we face in addressing a wide variety of abilities and needs in our college classrooms and how that makes our lives more challenging, it is difficult to imagine how gym teachers might possibly address the full range of abilities and interests in the classes they are assigned. We sometimes grow frustrated when the gap grows between the top student who we simply cannot fully engage as her mind wanders into more interesting territory and the lesser student who sometimes we must surely both wonder why he has chosen to go to college at all. Bridging this gap is difficult, and the best of us continually struggle with how to advance the class in a way that enables each student to get the most out of the course and take something with them when the class ends. Imagining the life of a gym teacher makes us imagine that it would be even more perilous. The gap between those with incredible athletic capital and those with little to no athletic capital would make the job of such an instructor quite an unenviable task.

Grant, a young man referred to in an earlier chapter, and who perceived himself as an athlete and who in many ways would have little in
common with Harold, nevertheless finds much about gym class lacking.
Despite the fact that he felt that he was able to perform the athletic and
physical demands asked of him, and he suffered no embarrassment, he
nevertheless viewed gym class as unnecessary, particularly given his
active participation in sports outside of school. Again, it seemed entirely
dependent upon the activity, whether or not a person in gym class
found it valuable or enjoyed it in any measure. Using these two young
contrasting individuals as a backdrop, it would seem that whether or not
you have athletic capital in large or small measure, and whether or not
you have an interest in athletics beyond gym class, the difficulty lies in
creating an environment in which both the athletically gifted and the
less athletically inclined can benefit in a meaningful way from the physical experiences. One thing seems clear: while Harold's lack of self-
confidence and lack of athletic capital made gym class seem like a
burdensome chore, Grant's athletic capital simply made it seem like an
unnecessary use of his time.

Kirk (1997) states two main problems with physical education
classes. The classes usually "treat [children] in the mass rather than as
individuals," and they require students to follow precise rules for body
movement directed by adults (44). The students who can participate in
the games or sports events using traditional athletic skills can reinforce
their athletic capital throughout their school career to gain status and,
in some cases, gain access to higher education. But the students who
may not be able to train to get their body to move in precise ways have
that counted against them in class and are often stigmatized. One side
note here to think about: we separate reading, math, science, and even
music classes according to students' comprehension and skills, but in
most cases physical education classes are not leveled—could this make
a difference in students' participation?

What has been observed and learned from our research, but also
discussed by all different types of educators, is that physical education
teachers interact and work with school athletes differently—it could be
seen in overt praise or asking them to lead stretches as well as in covert
ways like simply talking to them before class about sports, games,
classes, and so on. Even in schools where students can choose between
sports and fitness classes, fitness classes (which consist of using aerobic

machines) are seen as lesser. In fact, in one class that was observed, stacking and unstacking cups as fast as one could was considered a physical activity. This simply reinforced busy work for individual students and not body movement for students who did not want to participate. The message is: if you are coordinated, "you're in," and if you're not, this time needs to be filled with something—stacking cups may improve coordination, but it does not get one's heart rate up, which is often considered the baseline for physical activity.

According to Tinning (1997) "human movement" professionals are being trained in two different ways—one in performance and one in participation. Performance is more science oriented in how someone can improve their physical fitness level, "human performance"; and this is where more professionals are being trained, while few are trained in participation and how to teach to all levels (102–3). Thus PE educators are not being taught to teach physical activity participation but more toward performance-based teaching.

One parent interviewed commented (and we agree) that the people who chose to go into the human movement profession (for example, physical education or coaching) were most often people who were good at sports and/or found joy in participating. Most human movement professionals were athletes themselves—succeeding in physical education classes and participating at sports. They may not be able to help in a productive way or sympathize with the student who is having trouble in physical education classes. So it may not only be the more obvious differences in how a physical education teacher interacts with their students but the subtle ways too.

Sports and activities connected to schools also reinforce athletic capital. School sports have changed. Teams used to be open to everyone—and were even thought of as a social experience, as described by many parents who were interviewed, but that has changed. Children are being pressured into "specializing" in one sport as young as the age of four or five so that they can achieve greatness. No longer can a child try soccer at the age of eight or nine for the sake of trying a new sport because their peers have been in training since age five in order to be competitive.

Many towns now have recreation leagues and programs to start children early in sports. It is this situation that is a fine line between introducing children to recreation and sports activities and already scouting out these young people to play on elite teams. Christine, the mother of three mentioned earlier, explains that her town even has an introduction program to youth sports. She laughed while she was discussing all the opportunities open to four-year-old children. It seemed incredible to her that preschool-age children should be afforded so many options.

Athletic capital affects a young person's self-image, family, friends, schooling, and academic achievement. Through participation in sports a student receives praise from school, parents, and the community (e.g., local papers). In addition, wearing the team uniform reinforces his or her status. The school and community watch these students play in games and have pep rallies to cheer on their teams. In school, teachers know who the athletes are; in fact many teachers might even be coaches.

This status can also connect directly to the student's family. A parent can receive recognition through their child. Many people know whose children play on a sports team, and even more people know if a child is a star on that team. These can all be positives for the young person with athletic capital, but we have to acknowledge that this can also be construed as pressure to succeed. This elevated status reinforces athletic capital and makes it that much more important. The importance of athletic capital for children is played out in the lives of their parents as well. We, and others, frequently cite the importance of peer pressure and how that pressure influences decision making, both good and bad, among children and teenagers particularly. Peer pressure is also undeniably a factor in the lives of adults as well and goes beyond the old adage of "keeping up with the Joneses." For many parents their own worth is combined with the value of their children, and their perceived reflection of how they have parented those children. "For some parents, their adult pursuit of social acceptance and accomplishment is almost completely wrapped up with the achievement of their children" (Bigelow et al. 2001, 76). All of us are familiar with statements such as "Parenting is the most important job a person can have" or other variations like "Being a good parent is the toughest, most important job in the world." These statements parallel Bigelow's point suggesting that parents often perceive of their own self-worth largely through the accomplishments of their children. Those of us who are parents have been amused at times when we meet other parents who refer to us quite simply as "Ben's dad" or "Ellie's mom." Even sometimes after we've become acquainted, we are nevertheless referred to as the parent of so-and-so, and the reality is close behind: that we are so closely associated with our children, that we ourselves don't even have a name worth remembering.

All this praise for students who are good athletes continues the emphasis on sports, especially competitive sports, and today helps reinforce that one is either an athlete or not; but there is no participation in physical activity for the sake of exercise and fun for someone who does not have as much athletic prowess.

The lack of athletic capital negatively impacts the physical activity level of those who do not possess it, and this has cultural as well as health consequences. For example, in speaking with two sixth-grade boys—one in Ohio and one in Nebraska, both big football states—the boys would only throw the football around with their dads in their own backyards for fear of ridicule at school because they felt the they would get teased for not being able to throw well or well compared to their peers.

Another sixth-grade boy in Ohio knew he needed physical activity but just did not like gym class. In interviewing Joe, the difficulties he faces were borne out in his words, and the poignancy of the issues he faces should perhaps give pause to us all. While he is tall for his age, in fact the tallest in his class, he is also overweight. He does not appear to be interested in physical activity but does know it is important. His older brother is on several different school athletic teams. Joe acknowledged in one interview that he knew that he was supposed to get thirty minutes of physical activity a day. Knowing he needed to exercise but feeling the social need to avoid gym class as best he could makes his story more difficult, and probably a story shared by countless other young people his age. Why did he not enjoy gym? Because he didn't like the games they played at school (e.g., basketball). Instead, he likes games like tag. When questioned about this he said he doesn't like games that "have a point." Did that mean games that have a "winner or loser"? Maybe, but not necessarily; after all there are winners and losers in a game of tag too, but it just does not seem to be the same for Joe. Clearly, there is a big difference in what is asked of an individual in terms of skills for a game of tag versus a game of basketball. One can only imagine what gym class was like for the two boys who lived where college football is part of their state's culture. Chances are when traditional sports like basketball, football, soccer, and baseball are being pushed in physical education classes, boys like these are getting turned off, because at the middle school level they don't seem to have the same skill level as some of their peers. Problems become exacerbated then, as even the young people themselves recognize the importance of exercise, but struggle with feeling diminished if they engage in a sport in which potential embarrassment might follow. Most of us, we surmise, can relate to this at least to some degree, and particularly as we age, we may relate to it even more. For those of us well beyond the middle school years, there still is often a reluctance to exercise publicly, and for those who may need it the most, the problem becomes all too difficult.

In combination with America's obsession with sports, this sets up the power of athletic capital that makes it difficult for school systems to give attention to the importance of physical education for young people. Schools, as a reflection of our larger society, now tend to emphasize the importance of sports and being on a sports team rather than being physically active as a positive goal in and of itself. This is reflected in American public education where physical education is marginalized and/or cut from curriculums. Public education is supposed to be the great equalizer and within that system should be the education of mind and body. However, we are now seeing that students who possess athletic capital have access to sports through their schools (if they continue to have sports teams) or outside teams. But for the students who may not have athletic capital, there are fewer avenues to have exposure to physical activity. In another chapter we will discuss the ramifications of this stratified system of athletics on young people's health, but one can see how this creates a divide between those with athletic capital and those without. Consequently, as we have learned with culture capital, those who have more access to it gain more opportunities to build on it than those who do not; in the case of athletic capital, we are saying the same thing—what opportunities are lost to those who do not gain access to it by middle school?

WORKS CITED

Bigelow, Bob, Tom Moroney, and Linda Hall. *Just Let the Kids Play: How to Stop Other Adults from Ruining Your Child's Fun and Success in Youth Sports.* Deerfield Beach, FL: Health Communications, Inc., 2001.

Dyck, Noel, and Eduardo Archetti. "Embodied Identities: Reshaping Social Life through Sport and Dance." In *Sport, Dance and Embodied Identities*, edited by Noel Dyck and Eduardo Archetti, 1–19. New York: Berg, 2003.

Eckert, Penelope. *Jocks and Burnouts*. New York: Teachers College Press, Columbia University, 1989.

Ginsburg, Richard, Steven Durant, and Amy Baltzell. *Whose Game Is It, Anyway? A Guide to Helping Your Child Get the Most from Sports, Organized by Age and Stage*. Boston: Houghton Mifflin Company, 2006.

Kirk, David. "Schooling Bodies in New Times: Reform of School Physical Education in High Modernity." In *Critical Postmodernism in Human Movement, Physical Education, and Sport*, edited by Juan-Miguel Fernandez-Balboa, 39–63. New York: State University of New York Press, 1997.

Stevenson, Richard. "Confident Bush Outlines Ambitious Plan for 2nd Term." NYTimes.com, last modified November 5, 2004. http://www.nytimes.com/2004/11/05/politics/campaign/05bush.html?r=0.

Tinning, Richard. "Performance and Participation Discourse in Human Movement: Toward a Socially Critical Physical Education." In *Critical Postmodernism in Human Movement, Physical Education, and Sport*, edited by Juan-Miguel Fernandez-Balboa, 99–119. New York: State University of New York Press, 1997.

Welch, Willy. *Playing Right Field*. New York: Scholastic Press, 1995.

4

THE WIDENING GAP OF YOUTH ACTIVITY LEVEL

We are not the first nor will we be the last to lament the widening gap in the activity levels of our youth. Sedentary lifestyles and obesity have become a national concern. Our research has explored attitudes and habits related to exercise and physical activity in the United States. If you are currently or have recently been a parent of a middle school student, you may be familiar with the problems we've identified. You may also be understandably worried.

The data presented in this chapter is a blending of two research projects observing middle school culture. Many people from a variety of fields are discussing issues of youth physical activity, from obesity and health problems to youth sports, violence in sports, and screen time, to name a few. We will focus on three areas that contribute to the widening gap: (1) the increasing marginalization of physical education in the school curriculum, (2) the pressure on children to "specialize" in one sport at an early age, and (3) the widening gap between children who are privileged with athletic abilities and access to play and those who are not (this last point is also discussed in chapter 3, "Athletic Capital"). Other researchers have pointed out similar problems (Bigelow et al. 2001; Bishop 2009; Farrey 2008; Fish and Magee 2003; Ginsburg et al. 2006; Murphy 1999; Rosenfield and Wise 2001; and Sokolove 2008). Murphy (1999), a sports psychologist representative of this group, refers to the "dark side to youth sports" (9). He lists "burned-out teenage athletes, exploited athletes, troubled families, youth athletes with eating disorders, coach-parent conflicts, abusive parents—all are indicators of a deep and continuing problem with youth sports" (9). Our focus here is on the widening gap among these young people, and what that means for lifelong health.

THE INCREASING MARGINALIZATION OF PHYSICAL EDUCATION IN SCHOOL CURRICULUM

There are many reasons why physical education is marginalized in the school curriculum today. First, there is an increasing demand on school administrators to replace physical activity with classroom instruction. This demand is the result of federal policy such as No Child Left Behind, district budget limitations, teacher union contracts that limit working hours, lack of respect for the discipline of physical education and its teachers, the need for careful risk management as the United States becomes a more litigious society, and pressure to offer cocurricular activities seen as important for their school and students.

With public schools moving toward "teaching to the test," it becomes more difficult to provide school time for physical activity. Students, with their parents' help, are asked to make choices about what cocurricular activities they want to participate in. In some school districts the students have to choose among physical education, art, music, and other electives. At every school that we observed, students switched cocurricular activities each quarter or semester; only a few schools offered physical education all year long. Some schools are dropping recess or tagging on five to ten minutes of recess at the end of lunch.

Many teachers who teach cocurricular activities say there has always been a marginalization of cocurricular activities that hurts their disciplines at the middle school level. In most middle schools, students are grouped into teams that move through subjects or classes together. Team teachers work together as a unit; however, physical education teachers are not usually part of these collaborative academic teams.

Physical education is often thought of as break time for the teachers, and its teachers are regarded as "babysitters"—filling time while the real subject teachers meet or have planning time. It is thought that nothing is taught in PE; it is simply a way to burn off energy or fill time. Many PE teachers shared with us that frequently teachers take students out of PE to take tests, or they give students permission to go to PE late in order to finish a test—never thinking the students are missing something important or that students coming in late or missing class affect the physical education teacher's lesson plan for the day.

Maddie is a physically slight, eleven-year-old sixth grader. She lives in a city in Nebraska. She was dressed in jeans and a T-shirt and was very engaged in our conversation, the gist of which centered upon how certain courses in her school, called Academic Electives, were rotated through the week, rather than meeting on a daily basis. Perhaps it should not surprise us that some of the more "marginalized" subjects—music, shop, art, family consumer science, and physical education—were not provided a place on the daily schedule. Maddie explained her rotation schedule to us, which consisted of rotating times with different letters that were on different rotations than days of the week, but the gist of it was that on certain days when she has orchestra, she can't attend gym class. She added, "Most of the kids have either orchestra or band. I'm in orchestra so I miss out on a lot of PE classes. And it's only every other day so most of the time I miss out. On Monday I had PE but Monday is my orchestra day so I had to go to orchestra instead." If "most of the kids have orchestra or band" it means that "most of the kids" are missing PE classes.

A Minnesota school administrator, who has been in the teaching field for twenty years, told us that in junior high schools there, PE is becoming a choice. She explained that students get out of gym for numerous reasons; for example, parents excuse their children from gym to work on their grades. Parents often take their children out of PE because they believe that gym class is never going to be relevant to their child's academic development or, ultimately, to their child's career. This administrator also noted the pressures on children today to plan for college, even at the middle school level. Children need to prepare for college, she explained, and physical education "doesn't open doors"—which is ironic because many parents believe sports actually do open those doors. This puts a lot of pressure on children and parents to drop cocurricular activities such as PE, art, and music, unless of course the student excels at one. Even middle school students are already worried how their performance will impact their college options.

A physical education teacher in a large suburban town in Ohio reported that people there—teachers included—are encouraging high school students to take their physical education requirement in the summer. His students say summer PE is easy: all you do is run around and play some games. It is an easy credit. Having students take PE in the summer is reducing enrollment in the class during the academic year, so his school is dropping PE teacher positions. In fact, administrators are thinking about taking PE out of the curriculum altogether for ninth and tenth graders. He believes this is a way to start eliminating PE from the school system entirely, again a bit ironic given that we are hearing more concerns about sedentary lifestyles of so many young people. An art teacher in the same Ohio school system reiterated the gym teacher's concern that No Child Left Behind did not look at the whole student. It emphasized teaching toward the tests—focusing school curriculum on math, science, and English, but not on the physical well-being of the student.

In addition to the problems caused by the marginalization of PE, there are also inherent challenges for young people who do not see themselves as athletic. How do these young people learn to keep active? There are plenty of middle school students involved in school or community sports, but there are many who are not—and PE offers them an education about physical movement. Middle school PE is riddled with challenges for some students. Participating in gym class means "having to sweat," which means having to change clothes and shower in public. To a middle schooler in various stages of personal, physical, intellectual, and emotional development, those realities could seem to be very serious issues. Even college students quite vividly remember gym class:

> My school experiences with sports were both at the extreme ends of the spectrum. I went to public school until high school and PE was taken extremely seriously in both elementary school and middle school. It was really competitive and the teachers were extremely intense; in middle school we had to run laps on the track and we wouldn't get an A that day unless we got in at least a full mile. Elementary school had a lot of endurance running too and we were always graded more on ability than we were on effort (college junior, female).

This quote illustrates the importance of not discouraging children from sports as they work through this process.

The marginalizing of physical activity in the school curriculum may well contribute to the looming health crisis stemming from sedentary lifestyles and obesity. In this environment, students no longer learn that physical activity is a lifelong habit acquired in school; rather, the message they receive is that only competitive athletes need physical activity. Adults, in this case teachers, as the role models they are, whether they want to be or not, do not always teach and model the importance of lifelong physical activity. In the United States our public schools teach reading, writing, and arithmetic, but teaching young people how to move and use their bodies through exercise and fitness is largely ignored. Physical education shouldn't just be for athletes, or the children who are already good at sports; it needs to be there for kids who want to learn a new physical activity and particularly for those who aren't especially talented at sports, as they are the specific group for whom fitness and exercise could be an ongoing concern. Physical education is developing a reputation as being just for athletes, the children that are already active at sports, not for someone who wants to try or learn a new physical activity. As a result, physical education itself contributes to the widening gap between athletic and nonathletic middle school children.

THE PRESSURE ON CHILDREN TO "SPECIALIZE" IN ONE SPORT AT AN EARLY AGE

The pressure on children (and parents) to specialize in one sport, often beginning as early as age four, is also widening the gap between athletes and more sedentary kids. Children who start sports early and/or have parental support have a competitive advantage over those who choose (or have the choice made for them) not to start sports early. We heard many times throughout our research from parents and coaches that if a child is not playing a sport by age four or five they will fall far behind their peers. This attitude creates athletes at age four and leaves all the other children behind—which sounds pretty early to determine if someone would like something or not. It also seems, in many ways, somewhat ridiculous, given simple realities that suggest that short four-year-olds may become tall twelve-year-olds, and vice versa. "The most important thing adults committed to reforming youth sports can do is to put off selecting 'the best' and eliminating 'the rest' at an early age. We must abolish the youth sports caste systems that rank children according to their athletic abilities and entrap children as young as five" (Bigelow et al. 2001, 34). Thinking of youth sports as a "caste system" may be somewhat distasteful for our proclaimed more egalitarian society, but by now, any notion of equality in sports should already be very suspect.

One mother in Nebraska, where girls' and women's volleyball is big (the University of Nebraska is generally in the top ten), was worried that her daughter won't be able to play volleyball competitively in high school since she did not start at age five. "Parents are worried that their children will fall behind if they aren't engaged in as many activities, on as many teams, playing in as many seasons as their peers. Coaches worry that their teams will suffer if they don't practice as much as the competition" (Bigelow et al. 2001, 82). It has become an "arms race" (both figuratively and sometimes literally), and "unilateral disarmament" seems an unlikely option. In other words, many coaches and parents recognize inherent dangers in forcing sports specialization, but they are afraid that if they practice what they preach and really encourage their children/players to expand their horizons and try a variety of sports, that they will indeed fall behind those children who are specializing.

In Minnesota, it is said that if you don't start ice hockey by age four it is too late. This is making parents more conscious of what sports or activities they enroll their children in—trying to determine what their child will excel in at such an early age. For young children today, gone are the possibilities of trying lots of different sports or activities to see what they might like. Just as we see more specialization in the workforce, we see it with four-year-olds too. The notion of a "late bloomer" in the world of sports is becoming obsolete.

THE WIDENING GAP

As we discuss in chapter 3, one aspect of athletic capital is the availability of resources and parent/guardian involvement. This contributes to the same gap in youth activity. Having parents who are interested in sports definitely contributes to a child's participation. Caroline, a twelve-year-old seventh grader, from a single-parent home, recalls playing sports with her aunt and mom, who both liked sports. She says the reason she likes volleyball and basketball is because her mom and aunt "like sports." She had the opportunity to play with them and learn from them and in her words she "beat them." Caroline's mom also commented on her own involvement in sports while she was in school, and how she sees her daughter and her friend's involvement today much different than when she grew up. She sees her daughter as much more involved, but also understands some of Caroline's friends think she is too involved.

> Where I grew up we didn't have as much. It was a small town. I was in band in sixth grade because it was a small school. I did sports. I had a newspaper route on the weekends. I mowed lawns. I babysat. I know that some of her [Caroline's] friends are very involved and some think, "Why are you doing so much?"

Beth, who is thirteen years old, in eighth grade, and lives outside a city in Nebraska, was very aware that both her parents were athletes. She knew her dad played football and her mom was a state gymnast and was "super good." When she spoke she was clearly aware of her athletic lineage.

Another factor in being active is having parents who have time to dedicate to their children's sports. In the following example, two children are describing their level of involvement on teams—note that this means someone has to make sure they are on schedule, with workout clothes and uniforms, fed, homework done, and so on. Karen, an eleven-year-old seventh grader from Ohio, with an average build and blond hair pulled back, states:

> I have played volleyball since second or third grade. I did play on my school team and the season's over so then I play Spirit League [YMCA team] and my dad is the coach. And then I play a club team that does tournaments every Saturday. [Spirit] is mostly my friends. And this year for club I had to try out for a team so I'm with three of my friends but the other ones are on different teams so . . . they picked the team based on our skills. It was most stressful that way.

Henry, a thirteen-year-old eighth grader who lives in a Virginia suburb, competes on two teams. This is what his schedule is really like:

On Wednesday nights, that's where I swim [referring to a certain pool]. On Tuesdays, Thursdays, Fridays, and Sundays I swim at Pride Pool. I am on a club team; it's not a school team. Next year I'll be on the club team and the high school. There are a lot of kids on two teams, not really at my high school because not that many kids at my high school are also on the club team. So I will be in the water every day next year except Saturdays and twice a day on Wednesdays. That's what some kids do now. That's why I try to keep one day open so I can do some work. Swimming is all year round so you have to always do it even when you're not in school.

In addition, there are kids who at age twelve are practicing at 6:00 in the morning. Nancy is a twelve-year-old in seventh grade. She attends a private Christian school. Below she is describing her practice schedule:

We don't practice in the afternoons because the seniors and other demands on the gym so we actually do it at six in the morning. I get up at 5:30 in the morning. My dad actually goes to work because he has to be at his work at 6:30 so he drives me to practice. For basketball we have Mondays, Tuesdays, and Thursdays. And then volleyball we have Wednesdays and Fridays.

In Nancy's case it is fairly easy because her father can take her to school on the way to work and her mother takes her other two siblings, but for a family that does not have to rise that early, sports could not be an option if the ride was not available that early in the morning.

One thing that we heard from other researchers and parents alike is that overly involved parents are living through their child's sports experience. Some parents think their children will be awarded scholarships to college and make millions of dollars as a professional athlete—even knowing that only one in a million makes it to the professional level. It is not just dreams of scholarships and professional pay that drive parents' involvement in their kid's sport. If a child does well in a sport, it can bring recognition and status to the parents and family. Getting written up in local, regional, or even school newspapers is important to many athletes and the parents. A college student wrote the following in response to a question about participation in sports:

Our weekly school paper added fuel to the stigma that increased and better athletic ability equaled a high social class. Most, if not all of the articles published in the highly read newspaper featured storied athletes, their accomplishments, what universities they were being recruited by, etc. They rarely highlighted the accomplishments of students work in the classroom, unless they were Ivy League bound. Unfortunately, the students who perform well in the classroom tend to get swept under the rug while the students who can hit a home run or throw a touchdown pass received the popularity and attention from students, faculty, administration, and the town.

With social media, good athletic plays such as the scoring of a winning touchdown or an incredible basketball shot can go viral in minutes, and that can also bring recognition to the child and parents. Not to mention what is posted on people's Facebook pages in which the achievements of children compete with luxurious vacations for equal play. No longer do we simply get the holiday card from relatives listing the achievements of their children; now we get that news 24/7. The children who are not standouts, do not want to compete, or lack access to resources for athletic activity might simply stop playing early on because they begin to think they cannot excel in sports.

Christine, the mother of three active sons whom we met in an earlier chapter, discusses below why she thinks some kids might not participate in sports. It is interesting because this is an active sports parent viewing, and understanding, how other parents may not want to have their children involved in sports.

If you're talking to someone whose child hasn't been active, what is the stumbling block? Is it the fact that you couldn't get them to all the practices? Because if you have two working parents and a lot of the practices when they are little it might be hard to get them to practice. For example, earlier when I was working for the accounting firm before having kids I didn't necessarily leave the office until six or later. So would that be why some parents might not have their child involved at a young age? Because a lot of the time if they don't get involved at a very young age and all of a sudden they're ten and the kid hasn't done anything then either the kid isn't interested because it's not something he has done or the parents are just [saying] we never do that and they don't push it. We never pushed our kids into any sports; we just said, you know, "Do you want to do this?" And they always said yes. You've got some families that are almost the overachiever families where the kids are doing something every single day of the week. I guess the question would be if your child used to be athletic and is not, why do you think he stopped? And that would be the question for the child too. I mean did you stop because you just got so overscheduled and overbooked because you were doing too much? Or was it you just didn't enjoy it? Were your parents pushing you?

She continues by saying that some children might even self-select out of sports for various reasons.

With my own son Frank, basketball was his third sport of the big three that he liked to do. He always enjoyed it when he did it but did not see himself continuing with it. So we thought it was time to leave. There's a self-weed-out process, maybe not self but at the school because they only take so many kids. Schools have cuts. I forget how many kids tried out [for basketball] but fifteen made it. He's [her son] looking small on the football team now too but he's going to grow to be more like his dad and brother. He's got wide shoulders. He's not going to be as big as his brother I'm sure, but he's like 5'3" 140 pounds so he's not thin; it's not like he's going to get hurt out there, but he's shorter than a lot of kids. But for football he's still working at it. He might have always been one of the best kids and he's still good but there are other kids who are better because they might be faster because they're so much bigger now.

Clearly, Christine has thought about her son's involvement in different sports and has seen other children drop out or continue with a sport. She also brings up that school teams cannot take everyone and that kids are cut from teams, so it is about being better than others. She tries to be realistic about her son and how he physically matches up to his peers, realizing this could either help or hinder him making a team, such as being too short to play basketball but maybe being big enough to continue with football.

How parents view their children, realistically or not, impacts how their children see their involvement. One example that stands out in our research is the story of a Little League dad in Rhode Island who was helping to coach his ten-year-old son's team. On the first day of practice, one of the assistant coaches asked him, with all seriousness, how many boys on the team would make it to the big leagues. Reality suggests that only a few Rhode Islanders throughout history have ever made the major leagues, and far less than 1 percent of all Little League baseball players nationally ever make it to the major leagues. But when the first dad said, "Probably none," the second dad did not believe him. This is not an uncommon view. In her article, "Field of Dreams," Cristiana Quinn, who is founder of College Admission Advisors, writes, "Student-athletes—and their parents—can unwittingly harbor unrealistic expectations regarding where and how far their athletic prowess will take them post-high school" (Quinn 2012, 11). And because we live in Rhode Island, she goes even further by stating, "The truth is that because of its size, Rhode Island does not produce as many Division I athletes" (Quinn 2012, 12). Is the lesson here that we are in denial about our children's ability or that we are asking too much from our young children?

In big football states such as Arkansas, Nebraska, and Ohio, we heard many stories of parents who held their sons back early in school so when they entered high school they would be bigger than their peers. They hoped to give them a weight and height advantage over other boys their "age." We heard stories of parents keeping their children out of school an extra year, lying about their age to get them into a league that they feel is more competitive for their child's talent, and even hiring private sports tutors to improve their skill level. There are even private "academies" where athletes go at a young age to train in their sport. Ben McGrath (2012) in a *New Yorker* article titled "Head Start" documents several of these academies that have been in development for football quarterbacks (38–44). What really stands out is how young these players start—nine years old—and how these camps and academies have become their own industries, almost promising that they can make these youngsters into star quarterbacks (McGrath 2012). Many of these options come with a financial cost (travel teams, sports tutors, and academies), not to mention an emotional cost.

These options also contribute to children's loss of unstructured play because adults now organize much of youth activity. There are fewer opportunities for what we used to call neighborhood pickup games. This could be just nostalgia, but many adults talk about playing outside in their neighborhoods or on their farms for hours with friends. Neighborhood games taught leadership, handicapping, and dealing with rules and that a game is just a game. Young children who lived in the same neighborhood used to gather to figure out something to do—usually some game or variation of a game that they monitored and made work for their group. Now we have very few opportunities for children to do just that. For the children who are pursuing athletics, their time is now tied up with school and travel teams, practice and private lessons. The children who are not pursuing sports get the sense that only if you are good at sports can you play—the idea of a pickup game for fun seldom any longer exists. Gone are the days when neighborhood kids gathered in the afternoon and made up teams that seemed fair, handicapping for age and ability, and when no one really cared who won after the game was over. The good athletes don't have time to play, or they are worried about being injured, and the "nonathletes" feel like they should not even bother playing if they are not good. And sometimes, when kids do organize themselves, they are viewed with suspicion. An assistant recreation director in a Virginia suburban city shared a story with us about a group of youth wandering around a neighborhood one afternoon looking for other youth to play a pickup game of soccer. Someone who witnessed the young wanderers called the police thinking the group was a gang. The sociological implications present in such a story would seem to be significant, and so too do the unfortunate consequences. Sadly, it would seem that it has become such an uncommon experience to see a group of children together without adult supervision that we automatically think any group of such kids at best must be looking for trouble and at worst may actually be a gang.

In organized sport, the sport must become the child's, parents', and family's priority. Specializing at a young age is costly—financially, emotionally, and physically—and the growth of select and elite teams is widening the gap between those who can pay to play and those who cannot. The widening gap between children with athletic abilities and access to play and those without may come down to resources. In this section we examine more closely the resources one needs to excel in sports.

A child who wants to pursue sports needs more than encouragement. The family must dedicate finances for the child to participate in sports at the school level, in youth organized programs, and in the elite, specialized programs. We are talking about team or entrance fees as well as equipment, uniforms, gas money for the adults to transport the young athlete to different events, food money for both the athlete and chaperons when they are on the road and anytime a family dinner is altered for a young athlete, a hotel room if the games/competition are away, time away from work for an adult chaperon, money to run extra laundry cycles for practice and game uniforms, hosting team dinners, team photos and souvenirs, and the list goes on—all the extras needed to be part of a team. In addition to travel, select, or club teams, there are now Amateur Athletic Union (AAU) teams, which young athletes have to join because that is where college scouts are looking for their next talent.

An Ohio family with two boys (sixth and eighth graders) had to pay to play on public school teams: basketball and golf each cost $35 to participate, basketball team shoes cost $80, and for golf each team member must have their own clubs and balls. The school lends the team golf bags for their use during the season. One of the sons played on an Ohio Elite Travel Baseball team so there was a fee of $295 for that "privilege," which covered the cost of uniforms and other expenses. New cleats cost $40. A rough estimate of travel, food, and hotels added up to around $1,500 to $2,000 per season. This did not include having to take time off work to travel to the venues; it was assumed that using up vacation time was part of participating in this Elite Travel team. The parents interviewed were not aware of any scholarships.

Another parent pays $5,000 for his son to play on a Rhode Island Elite Middle School Soccer Team, while Rhode Island Little League fall ball is $85 and spring is $125. There are athletes who are recruited to play on "special teams" who cannot afford the fees, and there always seems to be a way to get these very talented athletes on the team despite their lack of financial support. But the majority of players have to pay to play. It has to be a priority for a family to use their resources for their children to participate in an organized sport. In addition, the parents/guardians have to have the ability and time to get their child to tryouts, practices, and games—not to mention seeing the child play in games. The online blogger "StatsDad" keeps a running tab of the money he spends on youth sports. In 2011 his family of three children spent $11,704 and in 2010 $9,076 (http://www.statsdad.com/p/youth-sports-costs.html). "We've come to equate spending on our kids' sports lives with achievement in sports. Conventional wisdom suggests that the more we spend, the more excellent our children become" (Hyman 2012, 3).

In the postscript of Mark Hyman's (2012) book, *The Most Expensive Game in Town: The Rising Cost of Youth Sports and the Toll on Today's Families*, Hyman writes that many of his leads for his book

> underscored the central message of the book, or the one I intended: that some companies and shrewd individuals have colonized youth sports in ways that have made them much more stressful and expensive, turning parents and even kids into consumers of products they had no idea they needed—or even wanted. In the end, what's for sale usually isn't eye black or such things. Instead, it's hope—hope that investing a hundred or a thousand dollars may advance a child's sports career just a little bit. And if it doesn't? Well, we've fulfilled our obligations as dutiful parents and given our kids every conceivable edge. (141)

This book and Hyman's other book, *Until It Hurts: America's Obsession with Youth Sports and How It Harms Our Kids* (2009), both caution parents of the pitfalls present in youth athletics. But are people involved in youth sports really going to change their behavior? Or do we all think we know what is best? We have convinced ourselves that "we" are not the crazy parent on the sideline, so we are impervious to the information that is out there. Two of Hyman's customer comments on Amazon reinforced this notion:

> The book, however, didn't really tell me anything that I didn't already know. If you have a child that participates in youth sports, nothing in this book will surprise you. Sure I learned about some new websites and services that prey on parents in the elusive quest for the college scholarship and there are plenty of stories about the extent that youth teams travel, but similar stories could have been accumulated at any youth soccer, hockey or basketball game. The extent that ESPN now covers high school sports will come as a shock only to those readers that don't generally watch sports on TV. (HoosierDadon amazon.com)

> Deep down, we know that most of our kids are not the next Ken Griffey Jr. but there's always that little gleam of hope that if they just had the right equipment, the right coach, the right experiences . . . they might exceed our expectations. They won't. But there are plenty of snake-oil salesmen who will take plenty of your money to encour-

age you to hold on to that hope and spend, spend, spend. While this book doesn't have a lot of answers, it does make you think about the questions: how did we let this happen? Why do we keep doing it? How are we reshaping our kids' worlds and expectations? (Mrs. Jennifer on amazon.com)

We are not sure what exactly HoosierDad was looking for in Hyman's book, but clearly he did not think this research told him something he did not already know. Mrs. Jennifer seems to be more reflective as she asks: "how did we let this happen? Why do we keep doing it? How are we reshaping our kids' worlds and expectations?" But the real question is: does it change how she parents her young athletic children? Sean Gregory's (2013) *Time* magazine article entitled "Final Four for the 4-Foot Set" sums up the dilemma for parents. The dilemma finds parents conflicted, particularly those who have competed in sports themselves, between their own recognition that such extreme levels of competition seem unnatural for such young children, yet finding themselves (and their children) seemingly enjoying the competition. He concludes his article by admitting that his seven-year-old son wants to play AAU basketball next year. Gregory writes, "Excuse me for a moment while I fetch a basketball. The devil is calling" (48). It would seem that Gregory's dilemma is common to many of us. In some cases, the dilemma transcends sports, as most of us do things that our gut tells us are wrong, whether it is eating too much junk food or not getting enough exercise, yet we continue to fail to do "the right thing." The dilemma as it pertains to our children also transcends sports as we sometimes keep our kids up too late on a school night for various reasons, even though we know they will not be at their best the following day. All of us do things that we inherently recognize as not in our own or our children's best interests, and yet we do them.

There are fewer opportunities to play sports that do not cost money or time, and those opportunities are not really accepted as "sport." It is getting harder for children to enjoy a sport only for the fun of it. Some sports are not offered through school or don't start until high school. For example, in Virginia a middle school student who loved to swim had to pay fees to join a club team because competitive swimming wasn't offered in his school. The many variables associated with involvement in youth sports factor into the decision-making process for most parents. For example, the father of a middle school student with whom we spoke, whose son is being recruited by both local AAU middle school basketball teams, is thinking of keeping his son out because of the expenses associated with the sport, not to mention the pressure and politics of it.

Sports teams are not only a place for children to play and have fun; they have become a moneymaking industry. The more involved a child is in sports, the more money the family will have to spend on heavily advertised shoes, equipment, and all the other necessary ancillaries associated with a given sport. Advertising influences people to a great extent obviously, and parents often willingly, and sometimes unwittingly, fall into the trap that requires only the "best" and most expensive sports equipment, training devices, lessons, and even sports drinks and nutritional supplements to be purchased.

The gap we are seeing in social economic status can be seen happening in the realm of middle school sports—the broader economic disparities are becoming evident in middle school sports. There are the obvious expenses but also unforeseen ones such as food, laundry, and team parties. There are costs in time too: travel time and the loss of time for athletes to do their schoolwork or contribute to the family chores.

We are already seeing some of the long-term implications of the gap in youth activity levels in high rates of obesity and diabetes, and in the percentages of inactive children and adults. In American culture we see being physically active and participating in sport as separate from lifestyle. Being physically active is something we check off our "to do lists," and participating in sports has become a stratified subculture of its own. Until we start working to have a better model for our young people, these problems will worsen. What skill set do we want our young people to have? What does educated mean? Isn't fit for life part of that education? Isn't that what PE is supposed to be about?

At the middle school level we have athletes competing on "select" or "elite" teams; at the other end of the spectrum we have a national debate concerning childhood obesity. Meanwhile, we are losing the middle ground. There is no longer a space for the child who just wants to be active or compete at a lower level. We are especially concerned with how this gap is hurting the young people who aren't especially coordinated. As these young people grow up, will they consider themselves unathletic? And those who lack access to the increased resources needed to be physically active—where will they be in twenty years?

Two sixth graders, one in Ohio and one in Nebraska, both said they liked to throw the football around with their fathers but not at school—they were too embarrassed to throw in front of their peers because they knew they were not very good.

Here are some questions that are being raised: We group students by ability into reading or math groups, but not physical education—what are the implications of that? We are living in a culture that is all about building self-esteem, but we seem to be unconcerned about whether our young people view themselves as being physically active. We are asking PE teachers to teach a spectrum of skills in one class—do we ask other teachers to do that? We don't have across-the-board physical education tests—why not? If we did, what would they look like? How can we create a more holistic view of education that connects the mind and body? How do we make being physically active a part of our life styles?

"How do we change it?" One educator explained that it is a long-term process that starts at prekindergarten. Middle school students (and their parents) are already worried about how their performance will impact their college options/choices. So, she concluded, we seem to be looking for short-term solutions: how can our children achieve in the easiest way? She correlates this search for a quick fix to bypass surgery; people choose it because it is easier than dieting. In fact, some insurance companies are opting to pay for it because it is more cost-effective than having clients who are unhealthy and overweight. But this does not address the habits or the culture in which people become unhealthy eaters, and it fails to address the real systemic problem related to lack of physical activity.

WORKS CITED

Bigelow, Bob, Tom Moroney, and Linda Hall. *Just Let the Kids Play: How to Stop Other Adults from Ruining Your Child's Fun and Success in Youth Sports.* Deerfield Beach, FL: Health Communications, Inc., 2001.

Bishop, Ronald. *When Play Was Play: Why Pick-up Games Matter.* Albany: State University of New York Press, 2009.

Farrey, Tom. *Game On: The All-American Race to Make Champions of Our Children.* New York: ESPN Books, 2008.

Fish, Joel, and Susan Magee. *101 Ways to Be a Terrific Sports Parent.* New York: Fireside Books, 2003.

Ginsburg, Richard, Steven Durant, and Amy Baltzell. *Whose Game Is It, Anyway? A Guide to Helping Your Child Get the Most from Sports, Organized by Age and Stage*. Boston: Houghton Mifflin Company, 2006.

Gregory, Sean. "Final Four for the 4-Foot Set." *Time* magazine, July 22, 2013, 44–48.

Hyman, Mark. *Until It Hurts: America's Obsession with Youth Sports and How It Harms Our Kids*. Boston: Beacon Press, 2010.

Hyman. Mark. *The Most Expensive Game in Town: The Rising Cost of Youth Sports and the Toll on Today's Families*. Boston: Beacon Press, 2009.

McGrath, Ben. "Head Start," *The New Yorker*, October 2012, 38–44.

Murphy, Shane. *The Cheers and the Tears: A Healthy Alternative to the Dark Side of Youth Sports Today*. San Francisco: Jossey-Bass Publishers, 1999.

Quinn, Cristiana. "Fields of Dreams." *Rhode Island Monthly's College Guide*. Providence: Rhode Island Monthly Communications, Inc., 2012.

Rosenfield, Alvin, and Nicole Wise. *The Overscheduled Child: Avoiding the Hyper-Parenting Trap*. New York: St. Martin's-Griffin, 2001.

Sokolove, Michael. *Warrior Girls: Protecting Our Daughters against the Injury Epidemic in Women's Sports*. New York: Simon & Schuster, 2008.

5

THE POWER OF PLAY

In this chapter we will examine the youth inactivity problem. One factor, we believe, that has contributed to the growing obesity problem among American youth has been the de-emphasis upon physical education. We would like to see a shift in thinking toward recognizing the interrelationship between academic achievement and physical education. Schools (and the larger society) must accept responsibility for educating the whole person if we are going to seriously address inactivity and the many negative things associated with a lack of physical activity and exercise.

First Lady Michelle Obama is personally taking on the challenge of ending childhood obesity in the United States. Her involvement in this issue allows for a tremendous amount of visibility that otherwise wouldn't exist. That exposure has already increased awareness of the seriousness of the issue. However, as we are sure Ms. Obama would acknowledge, this is not a new issue, but rather one that has been developing for a long time, and the solution is probably more complex than playing the video game *Dance, Dance, Revolution*. The popular video game, which was one of the first recommendations attributed to Ms. Obama by TV and radio commentators when she started her initiative in 2010, unfortunately focused attention back to the TV and away from more physical activities that she more likely had in mind. While the fact that the first lady informed us that the president is not apparently very good at this video game lent further publicity to the cause and contributed some levity to the situation, the real issue of the need for physical activity has been a bit obscured by the focus upon more sedentary pursuits. When playing video games (even active participation video games) becomes our idea of physical activity, one can imagine that the problems we face are potentially grave and long-lasting.

Recently Michelle Obama continued her fight by incorporating schools into her Let's Move campaign:

> Let's Move! Active Schools—an unprecedented collaboration to bring physical activity back to America's schools. The program provides simple steps and tools to help schools create active environments where students get 60 minutes of physical activity before, during and after the school day. Mrs. Obama called on school staff, families and communities to work together to reach an ambitious goal of engaging 50,000 schools in this program over the next five years. (http://www.whitehouse.gov/the-press-office/2013/02/28/first-lady-michelle-obama-announces-unprecedented-collaboration-bring-ph)

This is a good addition to her Let's Move campaign, but we still have a long way to go. We need to get all schools involved—not just the ones that can apply for grants and/or have one or two people who have the ability to spearhead an entirely new fitness program. There are different types of creative programs that are listed on the Let's Move website, but the programming needs to incorporate more children. We need to get everyone working with young people to contribute and buy in. What happened to the idea of educating the whole person, mind and body?

Currently there is much debate about what is happening to the health of our youth. We hear that things such as bad nutrition and excessive screen time are to blame for children's poor health, but we would like to make the case that we could begin to mediate this problem through a program we already have in place—physical education (PE). Most of the debate about education in the United States is focused on assessment and teaching to the tests. The No Child Left Behind legislation led many schools to focus primarily on academic achievement tests in order to maintain their levels of funding. The tests, then, became the school's main focus and "cores," "specials," and "co-curricular activities"—what we know as physical education, music, art, and industrial arts—took a backseat, unless enough taxpayer money flowed into the school and there was a principal secure enough in his or her job to continue to offer these other courses.

We have yet to really see what President Obama's Race to the Top initiative will bring to public education. However, the Race to the Top initiative, like education programs before it, has created competition between the states and between what is best for the state and education philosophies. And while these debates continue, schools are cutting cocurricular activities such as physical education—the part of the curriculum focused on teaching young people about fitness, health, and staying active. Public school physical education requirements remain only state mandated with no overall federal regulations.

On its website, the Let's Move campaign states that the goal is to work with the public and private sectors, and to work with the schools to improve school food programs.

> "I have set a goal to solve the problem of childhood obesity within a generation so that children born today will reach adulthood at a healthy weight," the text of the president's memorandum reads. "The first lady will lead a national public awareness effort to tackle the epidemic of childhood obesity. She will encourage involvement by actors from every sector—the public, nonprofits, and private sectors, as well as parents and youth—to help support and amplify the work of the federal government in improving the health of our children." (http://letsmove.gov/schools/index.html)

At first, the Let's Move campaign did not address physical education or play in the schools. The campaign literature points out that "many children consume at least half of their daily calories at school," but there is little written about "daily movement and physical activity" (http://www.letsmove.gov/healthy-schools). How long are these students sitting in school? The average school day is six and a half hours; multiplied by five days, that equals 32.5 hours per week (and there are 180 school days a year). That is at least one-third to one-half the waking hours of a school-age child. But what about working with existing physical education programs? The power of play is critical in teaching young people how to live healthy lives.

TOP-DOWN RESEARCH AND THE ROLE OF SCHOOLS

Much of the current research on obesity and health is being conducted from the top down, analyzing policy rather than talking to the individuals themselves: the youth, parents, and other adults interacting with young people every day—from physical educators to cafeteria workers to school administrators. Children in middle school are at a unique point in the enculturation process: beginning to understand and inquire about issues that pertain to their bodies and culture. This is when ideas and awareness of sport, physical fitness, exercise, and recreation start to come into their daily lives. At the middle-school age, individuals increasingly move to process and form their own identity; they become more aware of and pay attention to how other people look at them. This is a critical age to teach and learn about physical movement and health and to instill lifelong processes and habits that could lessen the many health risks associated with inactivity and obesity.

Do we ever ask the young boy or girl why they like or dislike sports? Or if they once liked sports but no longer do, what made them come to that conclusion? Don't most children like running, hopping, and playing with balls if they have the opportunity? At what age do they start to self-select out of athletic endeavors? "I feel that unequal opportunities and previous memories in gym class are two of the main reasons people choose to stay or leave sports. At a young age boys and girls are strongly influenced by their peers. It is through those memories and opportunities in school sports that many begin to define themselves as an athlete or not" (college senior, female). They may start thinking: "I am not good at soccer or baseball or even music or art." We have written elsewhere in this book about the role of the parent in this decision, but young people are also measuring themselves against their peers and maybe leaning toward activities that earn them praise by others.

> As a high school junior, I was hesitant to try out for the girls lacrosse team because everyone on the team was stronger and tougher than I was. This influenced my decision not to try out for the team because I was nervous I would make a fool out of myself in front of my classmates. I regret not joining the team because of the friendship and opportunities I missed. The appearance of this team held me back from trying something new, which I now think I would've enjoyed. (college first year, female)

How many unspoken messages are children receiving every day about being physically active? Has it become all about being athletic, and not about staying active? Somewhere along the line the joy of play has gotten lost in most sports programs today.

MAKING ASSUMPTIONS ABOUT PEOPLE'S LEISURE TIME

In many of these new fitness-type programs such as Let's Move, we are asked once again to make assumptions about Americans. Do all Americans have the leisure time and finances to support an active life-style—is it comparable to having the resources and being willing to make the financial commitment to eat healthy foods? Our neighborhoods and communities have changed in recent decades. There is little doubt that there should be a focus on better nutrition and less screen time, but as more and more parents are restricting their children from playing outside in their neighborhoods because of fear, would it not be equally or even more sensible and effective to upgrade physical education in the public school curriculum?

Almost every parent we talked with in our research brought up the fact that when they were young they would play outside for hours, until dark or when they were called in to supper. Their parents would not necessarily have any idea where they were. But today that does not happen; these parents, raised in the 1970s and 1980s, are not letting their children do the same. So these young people are playing indoors or with very monitored and restricted movement. Do we consider playing indoor games like Nintendo's Wii being physical active?

We already have a program in place to address children's need for physical activity—it is called physical education—but it has been getting lost in the educational planning, and No Child Left Behind really injured it. In fact, one physical educator we spoke with, in a wealthy suburb in Ohio, stated that he wished there was a test for PE because it would give the subject more credibility. The results of such a test could allow our political leaders, and parents for that matter, to see evidence of the poor health of many of our students, and upon seeing a clear need, perhaps measures might be taken to address the need.

There is an interesting history of physical education in the United States. In brief, it started with gymnastics training, movement activities, and games, but then shifted toward mainstream sports that highlighted competition. Today, there are debates about different pedagogical techniques and what should be the emphasis in this discipline. No matter what the emphasis, we argue that play is an integral factor in creating confidence and the willingness to meet the challenges of the increasingly complex roles required of a properly functioning adult.

GYM AND RECESS, AN EXTENSION OF PLAY

Most young children, no matter what their athletic ability, start out enjoying gym class and recess. Almost all our younger interviewees liked gym. This was especially true during the elementary-school years, but all too frequently changed in middle school. Some young people only take gym part of the year and find the inconsistency of physical activity diminishes its value for them. Others simply don't like the activities, and for many the new adolescent reality of dealing with a locker room and changing their clothes in the presence of their peers is understandably a very daunting process. A few even shared ideas about how to make gym better. For example, one student shared the simple but seemingly quite practical solution to many of the locker room difficulties: if everyone had gym at the end of the day then they could shower and change at home so if they got sweaty it would not matter.

For many, however, there is a major shift in young people's attitudes beginning in sixth grade—where most school systems group sixth, seventh, and eighth grades into "middle schools." Most physical education teachers already know what so many of us are only now considering: that somewhere along about middle school, curricular changes have shifted physical education and recess from something enjoyable to something to be avoided for many. Avoidance of physical education at all costs has become as commonplace in conventional wisdom as avoidance of high-level math has become for most students. This explains why so many adults remember their two "least favorite" high school experiences as math and gym class. While it may be more difficult to make math more enjoyable, the idea behind making physical education more inclusive for all and thereby more enjoyable for most seems, at least on its face, to be relatively simple.

In kindergarten through fifth grade, gym and recess is an extension of play. Many of the sixth graders we talked to had a hard time with the transition from having daily recess and gym classes at least twice a week to only having recess if you finished your lunch in time (amounting to about fifteen minutes out of a thirty-minute lunchtime) and possibly only having gym class part of the school year. Many middle school students who were interviewed discussed recess time or lack of recess time once they hit middle school. In many middle schools recess is tied to lunchtime. These young people have learned that you have to be in the front of the line to have enough time to eat and then have some recess time. Many kids strategize how to do this, but it is stressful to them because they have to weigh out where to eat, the line they are in, and how much to eat if they want to go outside.

What begins to happen is that sixth graders that enjoyed running and playing in gym and recess change as they go through middle school. Some of this is, of course, because of puberty and adolescence, but some is due to what we have chosen to emphasize in schools (tests). The culture that schools have created demonstrates the lack of importance attributed to physical education, and this is a major factor contributing to how our youth see physical education and the teaching of movement.

PHYSICAL EDUCATION SEEN AS BABYSITTER

Physical education is too often considered merely an add-on, a babysitter, or a place where students can blow off steam. Almost every physical educator we spoke with shared at least one story about another teacher, usually a subject teacher, asking if a student could miss or come late to gym class because of another class obligation or activity. This implies that the gym class is secondary to other classes or school activities and that it is okay to miss the class. That message is not lost on students. During one of our middle school observations in Maryland, a teacher asked one of the physical educators if a student could come late to gym because of a yearbook meeting—evidence, that in some cases, even extracurricular activities are seen as superseding what should be a curricular emphasis. Classes in middle school are typically no longer than sixty minutes but usually thirty to forty-five. By coming late, the student missed most of the class. Is working on the yearbook more important than attending a class, even if that class is "lowly" PE? Would this teacher have asked the same of a math teacher? And isn't it commonly understood that if you have to take your child out of school for some reason such as a dentist appointment, you do so during gym—what does this say to the child about the importance of this subject? The culture in the schools needs to change and the only way that will happen is if physical education becomes a priority and is seen as being as important as reading, writing, and arithmetic. This is especially true given the current obesity epidemic, which has serious implications for physical and mental development. A more active lifestyle is central to the development of a more physically active younger generation.

Why isn't physical education more important? Are we only interested in one type of education and not in educating the whole person? The United States is so concerned about test scores and how we measure up against other countries in a constant competition to be number one that we are losing sight of what is happening to our children physically.

EVIDENCE

There is increasing demand on school administrators to replace time for physical activity with classroom instruction. The priorities set by the U.S. federal government, district budget crises, union contract limits on working hours, risk management, and student choices between "cocurricular activities" leave little room for physical education in the curriculum. But there is mounting evidence that physical movement actually increases children's learning.

Dr. Walter Willett, physician and chair of the department of nutrition at the Harvard School of Public Health, who is well known in the field, says this:

> Incorporate physical education into No Child Left Behind. American children may be prepping like crazy for standardized tests, but they're seriously lagging in physical fitness. Regular exercise improves mood, concentration, and academic achievement. It can also help reverse the growing trend toward Type 2 Diabetes and early heart disease in children and teenagers. (Willett and Underwood 2010)

In addition, recent studies suggest that scheduling recess before lunch has changed student behaviors immensely, resulting in better eating habits and fewer behavioral issues (as well as fewer items in the lost and found). In addition, students are not hurrying through their meals to get outside to play. Teachers report that with physical activity students pay more attention and are not as fidgety (Parker-Pope 2010). Why has it taken us so long to realize this? Many parents already know this— having your child move around and play outside calms them down. Why would this not be the same concept in the classroom where we are asking children to sit for long periods of time?

A 2007 report entitled "Active Education: Physical Education, Physical Activity and Academic Performance" concluded, among other things, that more time in physical education and other school-based physical activity programs does not adversely affect academic performance. In fact, it was found that in many cases more time in physical education actually leads to improved grades and standardized test scores, through enhancing concentration skills and classroom behavior. The report suggested that additional research is needed to determine the impact of physical activity on academic performance among those who are at highest risk for obesity in the United States, including African American, Latino, Native American, Asian American, and Pacific Islander children, as well as children living in lower-income communities (Robert Wood Johnson Foundation Report 2007, 3).

In a report dated December 31, 2012, the American Academy of Pediatrics points out the importance of recess, citing the advantages of allowing a child personal time as well as many of the cognitive/academic, creative, social, emotional, and physical benefits associated with play (Council on School Health 2012). Even mainstream magazines such as *Parent* recently published an article entitled "The State of Play," which provides a short chronology of play and then gives parents some ideas of age-appropriate ways to "play" (Miranda 2013). While this is a great idea, it once again becomes something that is set up and structured, rather than play that is organic and unstructured. It is the ultimate irony; like "planned spontaneity," it seems oxymoronic to "structure" ways in which to achieve "unstructured play."

One of our sources works for a State Department of Public Health in New England. She said they are focusing on "built environments." These built environments create infrastructure to help with goals such as building sidewalks, promoting bike use, and aiding funding for parks. But this does not address PE in the schools. So while we do see states that value physical activity, many of the resources spent in order to promote that activity are put into areas that may or may not be utilized by young people, rather than into schools where they would most certainly be used.

These reports are only a few examples of the growing body of evidence that suggests that physical activity is increasingly valued as an integral component of meeting the goal of healthy and motivated young people who can go on to be engaged citizens. Thus we have experts saying one thing, but state and local governments who control school curriculums and funding are not addressing the issue. We see some cases where play and physical activity are built into the curriculum, but in many cases they are not.

OBSTACLES

There are local and regional programs to revamp nutrition in our public schools. Maybe we should also make it a priority to address how much movement schoolchildren should have during the school day. We need our school culture to stop marginalizing physical education and consider that this could be the starting point for training healthier children who will become healthier adults.

There seems to be an ongoing discussion about how much the student population is changing because of things like screen time: everything from video games to Facebook to Instagram. But guess what? It already has been changing. We are more diverse and have more needs. This is not something that popped up overnight, and if we know that, why aren't we changing the curriculum to change with our students? We are not just talking about getting iPads in the schools but to support new physical education curriculum in the schools and build environments that encourage a more active student body.

Several obstacles alluded to earlier in this chapter need to be overcome. First, the schools have to be dedicated to health and wellness. The administrators, especially the principal, have to be active supporters dedicated to health and wellness. The more marginalized that physical education and physical activity in schools become, the less likely that administrators are indoctrinated into a culture that puts a value upon physical activity.

Second, right now there is no room to increase the amount of time (days of the week, semesters, actual minutes) a student participates in physical education. The Centers for Disease Control and Prevention (CDC) recommends sixty minutes per day for children under eighteen (http://www.cdc.gov/healthyyouth/physicalactivity/toolkit/youth_pa_guidelines_communities.pdf). In many schools the students do not have PE throughout the school year. In a school in Rhode Island, which did have it throughout the school year, they only had one hundred minutes per week—far less than the CDC recommends.

Third, even though we believe it was not the intention of No Child Left Behind, the policy drastically damaged physical education in our public schools. As mentioned above the schools are under pressure to improve academic test scores. And without a "PE test" there seems to be little value if we cannot quantify our results. Also, in most schools there is no PE graduation requirement, though some districts are considering this.

Fourth, many school districts are operating in the red. In many districts across the country, there is little to no money to hire more staff or to pay teachers to work in after-school programs. In addition, the gap between wealthy and struggling schools is highlighted by the difference in wealth among and between school districts. Tax policy, in which schools are funded primarily through local property taxes, naturally favors the school districts with higher tax bases, which can spend more on equipment and outdoor space that promotes health and healthy living. Currently it comes down to whether families have money so they can "pay to play."

Fifth, union contracts limit working hours for teachers. One way to fit in more physical education might be to extend the school day. However, in Rhode Island, for example, the school day was extended in 2005 and teachers feel overworked as a result, making them less inclined to take on more duties and give up more of their own time.

Sixth, risk management—we have become a litigious society and that is reflected in our schools' play equipment and in which PE activities are allowed. For example, some schools even restrict how much running can be done at recess.

Seventh, and maybe the most important, is the marginalization of PE. There are problems with how some PE classes are structured and taught so we need to fix the school infrastructure first and then we can work with educators and curriculum. It is not a question of which comes first, academic courses or PE; if we change the thinking about PE and have top-down support, we will see changes in curriculum and teacher expertise.

At the beginning of this chapter we stated that there needs to be a shift, but maybe we need to work with something we have: PE in the public schools. Let's fix something that is broken (physical education classes) instead of going out and creating new programs that may not work. Yes, there are some bad PE teachers and not so good PE programs, but PE is already part of the school structure—our solution would not require creating anything new but making an existing program an important part of our children's education. There is important value in physical movement and educating the whole child: mind and body. We need to start demanding that our government put the same amount of energy into creating well-designed physical education curriculum as it does into testing. If schools had a mandate to focus on and support healthy activity the way they do with subject tests, we could have healthier and more self-directed children and adults.

WORKS CITED

"Adolescence Health and School Health Youth Physical Activity Guidelines Toolkit." Centers for Disease Control and Prevention. http://www.cdc.gov/healthyyouth/physicalactivity/guidelines.htm.
Council on School Health. "The Crucial Role of Recess in School." *Pediatrics* 131 (2013):183; originally published online December 31, 2012; DOI: 10.1542/peds.2012-2993
"Let's Move." http://letsmove.gov/schools/index.html.
Miranda, Carolina. "The State of Play." *Parenting Magazine*, July 2013, 86–94.
Parker-Pope, Tara. "Play, Then Eat: Shift May Bring Gains at School." NYTimes.com, January 25, 2010. http://well.blogs.nytimes.com/2010/01/25/play-then-eat-shift-may-bring-gains-at-school/.
Robert Wood Johnson Foundation Report. *Active Education: Physical Education, Physical Activity and Academic Performance.* San Diego: San Diego State University, 2007. http://www.activelivingresearch.org.
White House. "First Lady Michelle Obama Announces Unprecedented Collaboration to Bring Physical Activity Back to Schools." http://www.whitehouse.gov/the-press-office/2013/02/28/first-lady-michelle-obama-announces-unprecedented-collaboration-bring-ph.
Willet, Walter, and Ann Underwood. "Crimes of the Heart." *Newsweek* magazine online, last modified February 4, 2010. http://www.thedailybeast.com/newsweek/2010/02/04/crimes-of-the-heart.html.

6

ME FIRST

There May Not Be an "I" in Team, but There's a "Me"

The widening gap between elite players involved in team sports and their teammates at both the middle and high school levels has a variety of implications upon youth sports generally and individual development particularly. Labels attached to those who are invited to play at an elite level and those who are left behind, whether by choice or not, are often lasting. The enduring memories of our teenage years can shape our self-images long after we've left the school hallways and lockers behind. If media portrayals are to be believed, the reputations and images theoretically left behind at high school graduation aren't actually left behind at all, as they follow people throughout their lives and are revisited at reunions and other social gatherings. We cannot pin our collective desire to relive our youth upon the media, as many individuals can point to efforts to lose weight or otherwise look their best as they contemplate attendance at high school class reunions. It is surely not a "media creation" that our memories of ourselves and our peers in high school remain embedded in our memories long after we leave, and can influence our behavior and our perceptions of our own appearance and abilities years later.

Perhaps most significantly when it comes to the perception of high school as portrayed in the media, in Hollywood, and even as it plays out in our own minds, is the reality that for most of us, the "place" we occupied in high school was very real. For some, of course, that place was relatively exalted, and for others, that place was near despair. For most, there were good days and bad days, successes and failures, triumph and embarrassment, probably in mostly equal measures.

Memories remain, as do the gaps between those perceived by self and others as belonging to the in-crowd and the not-so-in-crowd. Just as those gaps remain among the popular and the less so, similar gaps remain between those who achieved a certain level of physical prowess and those who struggled on that front. Like the gaps between rich and poor, those gaps seem to be expanding. The differences between those who excel in sports and physical activity and those who do not are heightened by changes culturally in which high achievement leads more and more to exclusivity. While those who succeed athletically don't necessarily wall themselves off into gated communities as may those who succeed economically, nevertheless they often wall themselves off from those less able athletically in a variety of ways. Those walls are being built at younger ages than ever before, and the difference between those on one side of the wall and those on the other suggests that those walls may become even higher before they might be torn down, if they are ever torn down at all. The implications for young people, in which their society increasingly reflects the larger stratified society, are very real.

Those interested in sports have often lamented the ever-increasing disparity between high-level prominent athletes and "the rest of us." Perhaps nowhere is the difference between the "99 percent" and the "1 percent" more readily apparent than in sports. Professional athletes make huge salaries, stay in five-star hotels, fly in chartered planes, and generally live the life of luxury. Forgetting for the moment the work that has gone into this high level of success, there is a real disconnect (often loudly discussed on sports talk radio and television) between the athlete and the fan. Regardless of our love of sports, it is difficult to conceive of anyone in our society who has not considered this disconnect when plunking down significant money for a ticket to an event or for team merchandise for themselves or their children. The disconnect between pro athletes and the public is very real, and for better or worse, it is played out in social discourse in a variety of ways. We have come to accept it, while we may indeed lament the increasing disparity. But what about athletes who perform below the professional level? What about the disparity between treatment of college athletes (student ath-

letes) and the more general student population? What about the disparity between treatment of elite high school athletes and the more general
high school population? Is the disconnect filtering down?

ARE RECORDS NO LONGER MEANT TO BE BROKEN?

Recently, a young man in our state was lauded by the major newspaper
for breaking a sixty-year-old basketball scoring record for his school.
The story was significant for a few reasons. Breaking such an old record
obviously brings with it a nobility of accomplishment on its face, and
nobody should attempt to disparage such a feat, for it largely speaks for
itself. Still, one of the reasons the story stood out, and one of the reasons, at least in our area, why scoring records tend to stand longer than
we might expect, lies in a larger change in the culture of youth sports.
Culture change must surely be implicated, particularly given the ever-
improving training and abilities of many of our athletes. As training
becomes year-round, and specialization becomes the norm, it would be
only logical that records would be broken at an incredible rate. Yet,
records remain elusive, and when a record is broken, it remains newsworthy as a major milestone. It is possible that it is often less about the
inherent quality of the old record, than it is about the new reality that
many of our young athletes don't stay long enough in a given program
to break long-held records. Many young athletes with the ability to
break their high school's athletic records don't—not because they don't
perform at a higher level than those who preceded them, but often
because they simply don't stick around long enough. Some high school
basketball players now score their one thousandth point as juniors, and
in many cases would threaten long-held school scoring records, but
instead they leave for the greener pastures of prep schools, with better
competition, better facilities, better coaching, and better opportunities
to be seen. Whether these better opportunities actually pan out, or
whether they are more perceptions and less real, is, no doubt, dependent upon numerous variables, some in the control of the young athlete
and many outside of his or her control. Regardless of whether or not so
many of these young athletes *should* leave their homes and their schools
for the parallel universe of prep schools, the reality is that many of them

are, and the implications of that far exceed longer-lasting records in the school record books.

Some of us are old enough to remember when NBA superstar Earvin "Magic" Johnson left Michigan State (MSU) after two years. While many may argue that he was the best basketball player to ever attend Michigan State, he doesn't hold any all-time MSU records. Michigan State University's basketball website (MSUSpartans.com) lauds "Magic" and prominently credits him with leading the school to its first ever national basketball championship in 1979, but nowhere is his name mentioned among the all-time school leaders. In fact, "Magic" ranks thirty-fourth all-time in MSU scoring, just below Johnny Green and just above Marcus Sanders, names familiar only to ardent MSU fans. We've long been told that statistics can be misleading, and even in sports, it has been suggested that doing the "little things that don't show up in the statistics" is what a team needs from its players in order to be truly successful. Still, it is a relatively new phenomenon, in basketball perhaps more than the other sports, that the very best all-time players at major universities often don't hold all-time records as they simply moved on before the older records could be broken.

The same phenomenon of leaving early is even truer now as "basketball schools" like the University of Kentucky (UK) have become notorious for the "one and done" nature of many of their basketball stars. It is unlikely that any UK records will be threatened anytime soon, regardless of how skilled their new recruits surely are. "NBA ready" means that time playing college basketball may be measured in months, rather than years. The notion that many of these players actually fit the nostalgic notion of what a student athlete should be has become, in many places, simply a prehistoric belief as outdated to those of us in the real world as a typewriter is to those of us writing about it. While most athletes who attend college do so legitimately in pursuit of a college degree (after all, most research indicates that the graduation rates of student athletes is usually better than that of nonathletes), nevertheless situations like the one described above at the University of Kentucky make the notion that all college athletics are steeped in traditions of loyalty to the alma mater seem rather naïve at best.

Perhaps we must expect and accept such phenomena at the collegiate level, but we now find it creeping down to the high school level as well. Whether or not this falls into the category of "growing up too fast" is a matter of perception, but it is difficult not to notice that the pressures that accompany leaving home and going to a different school are not just pressures faced by graduating high school seniors anymore, but rather by more and more underclasspersons who feel the need to move onto greater opportunities prior to graduation. Sorting through the information overload that bombards many young people can seem impossible. Young athletes have to respond to their parents, their peers, their Amateur Athletic Union (AAU) coaches, their present high school coaches, future high school coaches, and others, and the information is often in complete conflict. Social media makes commentary almost immediate and must sometimes seem relentless. Opportunities to simply get away from constant criticism and/or commentary are rare and can only be achieved by those willing to isolate themselves in a way that is counterintuitive to the average teenager.

BEST INTEREST OR SELF-INTEREST?

Who can one trust? Who really has the best interests of the student at heart? Do AAU coaches really care about the young people they coach, or are they more interested in the connections they make with college coaches and others who may advance a particular AAU program? Are high school coaches really interested in the well-being of their charges, or are they more interested in the future of their programs both for appropriate and perhaps inappropriate personal reasons? We are all familiar with coaches who demand loyalty from their players but who themselves will leave at the first opportunity for a richer payday and a brighter future. It's hard to criticize upward mobility, but it's less difficult to criticize self-interest being masked as a concern for the well-being of others.

There is no doubt that some AAU coaches and high school coaches are pure in heart and motive and truly do have the best interests of their athletes in mind. But many do not. Even among those who do, the information with which they bombard teenagers making difficult choices can be so conflicting as to be more harmful than helpful. Parents have been told by college coaches that AAU doesn't matter and that the student should focus on their high school team. But if that were the case, why do the coaches seem to heavily populate AAU tournaments and seldom are they seen at a traditional high school game? AAU coaches tell their players that AAU is what matters most. High school coaches tell their players that high school matters most. Whichever view is more accurate, or whichever person speaks more truthfully than the others, is less the point than the reality that the voices in a young person's head are now far more real than they might have been in the past. The notion of "hearing voices" used to be a way to describe those with emotional disturbances; now it's simply a matter of trying to serve far too many masters. Personalities and self-interest can lead to very conflicting advice being shared with impressionable athletes and their overwhelmed (and equally impressionable) parents. We've personally heard of instances in which high school basketball players have been told by their AAU coaches that the AAU season(s) are much more important to the recruiting process than is the high school season. Others have said just the opposite. Regardless of where the truth lies, the implications of these confusing messages are huge. Should an athlete train harder for AAU season? When should they take some time off to rest those weary legs? Can they even consider taking some time off? Could they dare to play another sport in the "off-season" when there is no "off-season"? In extreme cases, such as we found in a few Ohio programs, and which are no doubt copied in many other places, even students as young as middle school were pressured not to play on their middle school teams and instead remain focused on their AAU programs. They were told that they could join their high school teams when they got to high school, but not to worry about their middle school programs. While this is a bit extreme given the age of the participants, nevertheless the message is clearly sent, and for those who were not elite, they were forced to sometimes painfully realize that the success they were achieving on their middle school teams would soon be ending, as the more elite players would return and join the program in high school. "Pain" comes in many forms in middle school, of course, and for some it comes in the form of not getting to play their chosen sport. For others the pain is more literal as more and more overuse injuries are occurring, particularly when young and still-growing athletes engage in repetitive tasks month after month and year after year.

Is it really harder to be a kid today? Everyone has heard that question and you've probably read articles printed in the mainstream and popular news magazines concerning the perceived loss of childhood for so many. Perhaps you've even pondered the issue yourself with friends over dinner. The answer, at least as it pertains to this chapter discussing the recruitment of young athletes, is, in our view, unequivocal: the answer is yes. It is indeed more difficult to be a kid today, especially if that kid is a talented athlete who must weigh a variety of conflicting interests in determining how far they might be able to pursue their given sport(s). Pressures from within the child's family and those from outside exerted by coaches, peers, and even other parents can seem insurmountable. Often, even though parents don't intend to exert pressure, the child nevertheless senses parental pressure. Even well intentioned remarks intended as compliments or confidence boosts can be taken as heightened expectations. It becomes, in some ways, a catch-22. Instilling confidence in one's child, a concept that few would criticize, can become, in the child's mind, a parent's desire for that child to pursue a sport with more vigor than they might have otherwise wanted. What is a parent to do? It's difficult to imagine that tempering a child's dreams would be more appropriate, but still, without such tempering, pressure builds. When can we be fully certain that a child's desire to pursue a dream of becoming a better and more elite athlete was fully the child's dream and not the child's perception that they must fulfill the dreams of one or both parents?

Think of the young man who is a gifted ice hockey player. The need for ice-time and the expense of travel to that ice and to the many tournaments involved often means that there is a clear line of demarcation between the young athlete who plays high school hockey for fun and the young athlete who may have a realistic shot at a college scholarship or an even higher future in the game. Kids often are "forced" by many outside influences to leave home at relatively tender ages. They are frequently taken in by other hockey families who can care for them while they work on improving their hockey talents while attending classes and growing up far away from their families. Something that seems to have been a relatively common occurrence in Canada has begun to spread to the United States, as kids leave their families to get better coaching, play on better teams, and generally get the notice of college coaches and others who simply would not have noticed them if they had stayed with their high school teams. (The thought of young people being shipped away from their families to receive better coaching and to play on better teams was once the exclusive province of

Communist countries, or Olympic athletes more generally. We now all have seen the human-interest stories so prominent during the Olympic games of young gymnasts who are sent away to train with experienced coaches. We celebrate their resolve and their courage and their willingness to sacrifice. While Olympic athletes remain exceptional, the once quaint notion of being sent away at a young age to become a sports specialist has become far less an exceptional case.)

IS IT PLAY OR IS IT WORK?

Hockey players and gymnasts are not the exception any longer. The same phenomenon is true (if to a slightly lesser extent) for basketball players, particularly in the northeast, who feel compelled to trudge off to elite prep schools to ply their craft, under the watchful eyes of (probably) more able coaches who are (certainly) more connected to college programs and others whom the young athlete yearns to attract. Whether or not these young teenagers are truly ready to leave home and go off to boarding school becomes less relevant than the requirement that they get themselves in better situations for the recruiters to notice them. At some point "playing" the game has become "working" the system. The irony of making play become work is not lost on the two authors of this book, who, like so many people we hope, have the luxury of doing what they love to do for a living; a luxury that seems all too "grown-up" in today's world in which kids must forgo play in order to work at their craft. It would be hyperbole indeed to compare the work of today's young athletes with the sweatshop work that many people their age engaged in a century ago. Nevertheless, sometime between that era of forced and unforced child labor and today's hyperdependence upon focused practice and limited play, childhood may have largely been lost.

Students who might want to play another sport, even for the fun of it, often feel compelled not to do so, as they must focus all energy upon their one sport. One young man we interviewed and have followed wanted to play baseball and was rather skilled at the game, but since basketball was his sport, his AAU coaches as well as his prep school coach discouraged him from playing even two months of baseball. He was told that spring (after the high school season had ended) was the most important time to be seen by basketball coaches and he wouldn't play as well in front of them if he didn't entirely devote himself to basketball. That may or may not be true, but what is certainly true is that baseball then becomes a spectator sport only for this young man. Will that be the best thing for his future?

Earlier in this chapter we touched upon the notion that the difficulty of the choices now facing elite athletes contributes mightily to a culture in which they must simply grow up too fast. The "hyperfocus" upon one sport to the exclusion of all other activities leads to a specialization mentality that contributes to this phenomenon as well. The pressures that this particular young man faced that almost literally forced his hand into dropping baseball from his activities list surely contribute to an atmosphere in which pressure is always present, and "fun" is reserved for those with lesser talents. Imagine the courage it would take for the young man to stand up to the pressure and insist on playing baseball for the fun of it. Imagine if he stood up and played baseball and didn't have a good spring basketball season. His AAU and high school coaches would be well prepared to tell him that they had "told him so," and that the lesson for others should not be lost. Would it be because he played baseball? The fact that we wouldn't really know is less important than the fact that he'd be told that was the reason, and his obvious "lack of devotion" to basketball led to a lessening of his skills in that sport.

We have thoroughly evolved (devolved?) from an era in which most of our truly gifted athletes played numerous sports into an era where the notion of three-sport stars or even two-sport stars will all but be forgotten. We used to worry about college coaches who seemed to "own" their players and controlled their time out of class (sometimes in class) to the extent that college athletics became a burden and a curse more than a joy. Now, perhaps the same can be said for coaches of athletes at a younger age. Do high school coaches "own" their players' time? Do prep school coaches? Perhaps if a student chooses to attend a prep school and move from home to do so, they should have a full understanding that their time is no longer their own, but do they? Should they if they are not even of adult age? That college coaches "own" their players' time has, in many circles, become conventional wisdom. Abuses that follow have been well documented. The *Newark Star-Ledger* published a critical account in 2013 of the actions of Seton Hall's softball coach, who, apparently at least, forced her athletes to place softball far above family and school, and punished those who couldn't or wouldn't conform to her standards, by benching them, suspending them, or otherwise sending the message that softball must come before all else (http://yahoo.com/blogs/the-turnstile/seton-hall).

The idea of playing for fun is often lost entirely. Certainly in the larger high schools and programs where the teams are highly competitive, the notion of someone going out for a sport just to have fun, as perhaps their parents may have done years before, is now some sort of absurd fantasy. A young person playing a sport for fun would either likely be cut from the team or never see a minute of playing time, as playing time is reserved for the serious athletes who've devoted themselves to this sport. One possible side-benefit does occur for a select few "middling" athletes: those who now actually do receive playing time on their high school team because one or two of the truly elite players have gone on to boarding school, thus opening a slot for them. But even noting that benefit, the seriousness with which we now approach high school athletics in many cases has made for an environment in which playing for fun seems as distant as going to college to learn about life rather than to prepare for the workplace. Pressure mounts to receive scholarship offers; and it feeds a culture in which to be good at sports suggests that there must be a scholarship offer forthcoming, and for those without offers, the perception becomes that they simply aren't good enough.

It may also be worth noting that we often abdicate our decision making as parents and allow children as young as fourteen or fifteen to make major decisions concerning where they will go to school, where and with whom they will live, and even what lifetime interests they will pursue. Sending a child off to prep school or to live with another family as the child pursues his or her athletic goals means that parents necessarily lose much of their day-to-day influence. If you re-read that sentence you might be thinking (as are we) that it is probably not a good idea to allow teenagers to make such major life choices. These are, after all, the same young people who have to be told to pick up their towels from their bedroom floors and to wear a coat when it's cold. How can we be entrusting major decisions to people who are sometimes closer in age to believing in Santa Claus than knowing how to live on their own?

Given the costs of higher education and the necessity for that education in today's economy, the pressure to get there has increased seemingly exponentially. Just one or two generations ago, parents viewed college for their children as the way toward upward mobility and as a source of family pride that went beyond other more tangible assets. Today, it is less about family pride and upward mobility than it is about maintaining one's economic place at the table and not falling too far behind. The pressure faced by parents has clearly affected those parents' views of the necessity of college for their children, and children who are gifted enough athletically might view those gifts as every bit as much a curse as a blessing. For some parents, a college scholarship for their children may very well be an economic necessity, and absent such a scholarship, there simply won't be college in that child's future. For others, it has become not so much a necessity as another luxury to pursue. Either way, whether for economic necessity or perhaps to attain less noble ends, sending a child off to prep school in order to expand his or her opportunities (and to increase his or her visibility in the college recruiting wars) changes the manner in which we parent, and clearly, the way in which we pressure our children, both consciously and subconsciously. Those of us who have made the difficult decision must struggle with our own knowledge of our individual abilities to rationalize the decisions we make. Did we truly send our son off to prep school so he could attain a college scholarship and thereby make our lives easier, while making his more difficult? In a nutshell, did we send him away to pursue our dreams? Or, in contrast, did we send him away for all the right reasons: better opportunities, better facilities, better chances to pursue his own dreams?

Whether the difficult decisions are made for the right or the wrong reasons, and/or whether parents or child can objectively judge whether the decisions were made for the good of the child or not, there can be little debate that sending a child away from home necessarily changes the relationship between parents and child. Parents have long prepared themselves as best they can for the day their child leaves for college or some other venture upon graduating from high school. Changes that such freedom creates in the child are sometimes viewed with great pride by the parents and other times with a certain level of horror. Mistakes are made, lessons are learned, and maturity is achieved. But for those who are gifted at sports and who are sent away at a younger age, many questions about their readiness for that level of freedom remain. Mistakes are made, lessons are hopefully learned, maturity is hopefully achieved, but only if the child is actually ready to learn from his or her mistakes and accept those lessons that should be learned, and grow into that maturity that otherwise naturally comes with age alone.

One young man on a basketball team was a relatively late arrival as a junior into the program, and as such was not on the radar of a lot of coaches who look to the prep schools as one feeder into their programs. As a result, he was looking forward to the many coaches who would be attending practices and games because of a highly recruited teammate. Unfortunately, the teammate committed early, and thus, all of those coaches who would've seen this young man play no longer needed to attend practice and no longer would "accidentally" see others on the team. In and of itself, such a story isn't a big deal, but the disappointment and the pressure felt by the young man I've described were palpable. "To see and be seen" used to be a motto more appropriate for social outings, rather than high school athletic arenas, but the pressure of looking good so that others might see you now follows young athletes from practice to games and beyond. Many parents try to balance the appropriate interest in their child's progress with the need to relieve pressure placed on that child from both external and internal forces. Children aren't just watched by prospective recruiters who may attend the occasional game, but also by coaches who are invited to practices to get a closer look at someone in whom they have interest. The pressure mounts as the young athlete must perform well even at practice, and especially if a coach may be watching. Allen Iverson's famous "We're talking about practice" line changes radically in this context, in which young athletes have little to no freedom to work on their games or practice their weaknesses, as they surely feel compelled to compete at the highest level and impress whoever may be watching. The implications that this has upon the team and the team concept are obvious. "Me first" becomes "me only." Another aspect that gets lost is the lessons learned about teamwork, loyalty, and pride. There is less a need for school pride and all that accompanies it, as the young athlete is forced to worry more about where they are *going* to play rather than where they *are* presently playing.

Parents on the sidelines also can affect team loyalty as well. Most of us are familiar with the "child first" parent, who we suspect must surely contribute to the "me first" child. Parents who cheer for their child rather than the team are becoming commonplace in the gymnasiums many of us frequent. We have been in gyms and in the bleachers at football games where parents are filming their children on the field . . . not the game itself, but *their* children on the field. In other words, if one's son happens to be playing on the defensive line, the camera focuses on him alone and thus where the ball is or what is actually happening in the game is irrelevant. Some of these parents can attend every game and have little idea how the team is really doing, but they have an excellent idea of how their son is doing. Parents can be forgiven for taking a greater interest in their own children than in all the children, but can they truly be forgiven for taking "only" an interest in their own children? Would it hurt them to cheer for the team now and then or for another player after he or she makes a great play? Whether it would or not becomes moot, in a culture in which the idea of watching only one's child and cheering only that child becomes the norm rather than the exception.

There is also the increasing concern (more fully explored in our "Little League parents" chapter) of parents' behavior on the sidelines and the embarrassment that can cause young people playing the games. Sometimes that embarrassment is coupled with extra pressure added to the child as the parents' level of frustration with the level of play or officiating or coaching becomes an added burden placed upon an already highly stressed participant. While a parent who shouts at a player, coach, or an official may not even be heard by the target of the derision, that parent should be aware that his or her son or daughter can and does tend to hear it. A 2012 CBS survey suggested that fully one-third of American kids between the ages of eight and fourteen who play sports wish their parents (or any adult for that matter) would not watch. "They say the adults yell too much, are distracting, make them and teammates nervous, put pressure to play better and win, and just plain old make the kids feel bad" (CBS Miami, 2012). It is possible, of course, that the "exceptional" athletes who attend prep schools to improve their performances and their standing don't all feel the same way as more typical eight- to fourteen-year-olds do; still, it is perhaps worthy of our consideration that children are highly cognizant of what their parents are doing, what their parents are saying, and the effect that those words and actions are having.

Many parents have officially evolved from cheerleaders for their children and their children's teams, to de facto coaches muddying the already clouded waters that their children are attempting to navigate. Hyman (2009) referred to these parents as "overly invested" and as a "part of the game to be overcome, like zone defenses and shoelaces that won't stay tied" (115). As children grow older and graduate from the youth soccer games so prevalent throughout the suburban United States into their specialty sports, the investment that parents make becomes even greater. While much of that investment is financial, the more significant investment is time, and most significant investment is the emotional investment that many parents make. It is one thing to want one's child to do well and achieve his or her goals; it is quite another to live through the child to such a degree that the parent takes on coaches, referees, and others who might stand in the way of success that the parent feels is either being unrecognized or unrewarded. Keeping the young athletes focused becomes more difficult as the child must worry about what their parents may do on the sidelines or what they may say to the coach or referee.

Again, we return to the concept that young athletes must grow up too fast. In this case, they must sometimes assume the role of parent themselves and comfort their own parents after a particularly difficult loss or a game in which they didn't play well. Many of us have been witness to scenes after a loss in which the parents seem angry, despondent, or some combination of both, while the child who has suffered the loss directly is able to move on quite well almost immediately. This isn't only true of younger children who move on to their juice boxes and snacks provided by the parents on the sidelines; it seems to also remain true for older children who know quite well how they've performed and are already beginning to move forward while their parents continue their postmortems long after the game has ended.

It is not difficult to imagine the young person's stress entering a game, in which they not only must concern themselves with how they play in order to please their coach and whatever other coaches for the future may be watching, but also their realization that if they don't play up to par, their parents may be waiting for them after seeking "explanations for their poor play." The days of "you'll get them next time" and "you did your best" are replaced by "if only you had done this" and "why didn't the coach do that?" In defense of parents, saying and doing the right thing isn't altogether easy. Navigating the fine line between constructive criticism and damaging diminishment parallels the other line between effusive misplaced praise and appropriate encouragement. Of course, that fine line is also continually navigated by parents whose children are not involved in sports; finding the right balance between proper encouragement of a child who shows an interest in art or music, or academics in the more traditional sense, and simply unrealistically praising a work product that shows little such promise is the difficult role of a parent. Knowing when to prod and "demand" more effort and knowing when to back off and simply praise a job well done is more an art of parenting than it is a science.

Parents who tell their children how exceptional they are and sometimes even reward their children, monetarily or otherwise, not for team victories, but for points scored or other individual statistics, also contribute to the lessening of team loyalty. We've been made aware of parents who monetarily reward their own children when they record a sack on the football field or score points on the basketball court. Such incentives certainly encourage a young person to shoot rather than pass on the basketball court, or to take risks on the football field in order to make great plays rather than play within the confines of the team structure. Even coaches, who may preach the virtues of team play, tend to accentuate individual accomplishments such as points scored and big plays made over less glamorous team-oriented goals. Is there really a reward in being a team player in such an environment? At the risk of stating the obvious, however, it is not just in the sporting realm where individual accomplishments are rewarded beyond their contribution to team success; many parents who might show disdain for a parent who rewards a child for how many points they score in a game might be quite comfortable with paying their own child for good grades. In a results-oriented society, it is easy to become obsessed with good grades (beyond good learning) and in points scored (beyond team success).

In years of watching basketball one "me first" happening has become so ever present that it has become a part of accepted and conventional wisdom. Even though it's so clearly wrong, and would likely make Hall of Fame coach John Wooden roll over in his grave, it has become so commonplace that we don't even challenge it anymore: we speak of the final seconds in a close or relatively close basketball game, in which the trailing team must foul in order to get the ball back. Even at an early age now, many players interested in padding their statistics, beyond winning the game, have taken to holding the ball and taking the foul

rather than passing to a wide-open teammate and taking precious seconds off of the clock. If you've watched basketball as we have, it's
difficult not to notice such a trend, and the only real explanation for it
has become the importance placed upon individual statistics. We have
watched countless games that could have ended much sooner, had the
person with the ball passed it to an open teammate rather than cradle it
like an infant awaiting the foul to come that will put them on the free
throw line. Announcers have come to accept it with such fervor that
they sometimes even commend the intelligence of the player who waits
for the foul to come, rather than dribbles or passes away from the
opposition. Obviously, we aren't suggesting risky passes or passing to a
player who struggles making free throws, but all too often wide-open
players are left wide open while the player with the ball holds it until he
or she is fouled. It defies basketball common sense, but it has become
basketball conventional wisdom.

While most coaches still frown on taking a last-second shot (when
one's team is ahead), even that sacred cow is becoming endangered.
The increased emphasis placed upon individual accomplishment becomes ingrained in young people who increasingly play sports to somehow "get ahead in the future" rather than win the game in the present.
Perhaps increasing the emphasis given to assists and rebounds and other statistics could lessen the importance placed upon scoring points
alone. While relatively new terms such as "double-doubles" and "triple-
doubles" have arisen and do seem to increase the emphasis placed upon
statistics beyond scoring, much could still be done to improve the team
culture and de-emphasize the increasing individualism associated even
with team sports. Again, using basketball as the example, almost all high
schools report scoring records and scoring totals for their games. Far
fewer report rebound totals and/or assist totals. If a young person wants
to see his or her name in the local paper, he or she had probably best
lead the team in scoring, rather than in assists.

Such hyperemphasis on the future, rather than the present, and
upon individual achievement and acclaim, may explain an equally trou-
bling phenomenon: the "unhappy winner" and the "happy loser." We've
all become accustomed to children who are unhappy even after their
team wins because they simply didn't play well and its corollary, children who are happy even after their team loses because they personally
performed well. Gone for many are the days of team victories and team

losses in which it didn't matter how the individuals played, as long as the team came out with a victory. Now winning may not be enough, and losing may be just fine—it all depends on how the individual played. It is difficult in such an environment to preach the virtues of teamwork and collective action, and nearly impossible to expect young people to extol those virtues.

Anecdotes, while useful, merely depict one snippet in a much larger story. The larger story centers upon the pressure that young student athletes feel as they seek the affection of recruiters. There is, of course, the pressure that parents put upon them, and certainly more anecdotes could be relayed concerning the off-the-wall antics of some parents in that regard. While some parents are clearly over the top with regard to pressuring them to excel in sports, still others seem to have gained the proper perspective. Still, even for children whose parents don't overtly pressure their children to play well in front of recruiters, there remains a certain covert pressure in which children know the money involved and the sacrifices their parents have made with regard to travel, league, and coaching expenses, and many young people internalize that pressure to their detriment as well. Unfortunately, the old adage of "play well with others" has translated into "play well in front of others," and individual achievement and accomplishment trump team goals.

WORKS CITED

CBS Miami. Poll: Kids Don't Want Parents Watching Extracurricular Sports. March 27, 2012. http://Miami.cbslocal.com/2012/03/27/poll-kids-dont-want-parents-watching-extra curricular-sports

Hyman, Mark. *Until It Hurts: America's Obsession with Youth Sports and How It Harms Our Kids*. Boston: Beacon Press, 2009.

7

THE LOSS OF COMMUNITY THROUGH SPECIALIZED SPORTS AND THE LOSS OF UNSTRUCTURED PLAY

The chapters in this book have integrated several concepts and themes, including chapters concerning helicopter parents, children playing on a team their parent coaches, and obviously the relationship between sports and popular culture in a variety of contexts. In this chapter, we consider the concept of unstructured play and the ways in which that play has been addressed in popular culture, by using movies, television, and other popular media as a lens through which we view the portrayal of children's play in the past and the differences we see with how children play today.

A vivid example, at least for us, of the way in which the very nature of play has changed is seen in the movie *The Sandlot*, produced in 1993 and set in 1962, about a group of fifth graders who get together every day in the summer to play baseball. In one of our classes in which sports was a focal point, we used *The Sandlot*, among other films, to illustrate the evolution of play across the years. Students not only enjoyed studying the concept, as well as considering their own experiences with structured versus unstructured play, but they really enjoyed the movie itself. Perhaps some of that enjoyment centered around the nostalgia that *The Sandlot* portrayed, while remaining current in the sense that students could relate to some of the dilemmas the young boys faced. The nature of the relationships among and between the boys and the other characters in the film, including the "new kid's" mom and stepfather, also seemed to resonate with many of the students. The movie had attained a certain cult following long before its use in one of our classrooms, and our experiences suggest that even those who had previously watched the film as entertainment could also benefit from discussion and consideration of the many social issues portrayed. Once word of mouth spread, students wanted to watch *The Sandlot*, and it became a cult phenomenon in our classroom, just as it had been in larger society, in which students wanted to watch the film over and over. Some even were able to respond to each scene and memorize important dialogue. The status of *The Sandlot* as an enduring film has been seen in the year 2013 upon the twentieth anniversary of its release, when it has been featured in a variety of settings, including having been shown in at least one major league ballpark upon the completion of a regularly scheduled Major League Baseball game.

The movie romanticized our nostalgic notions of utopia in the suburbs—a place where people didn't lock their doors when they left the house and where going down to the playground or to the vacant field to play involved only the concern of losing the baseball or skinning one's knee. The depiction of a community might seem somewhat out of place or at least idealistic in today's world. While parents had their concerns about their children growing up in the 1960s, those of us old enough to remember that era remember a far different time. A time in which the thought of wearing a bicycle helmet or even a seatbelt as we rode in the family car (however smart those choices obviously would have been) would not have been considered. Even more grave concerns about predatory adults and bullying children would have seemed very remote.

Today, obviously, parents, and subsequently their children, have larger and more serious concerns when they leave the house alone. In some neighborhoods, parents quite rightly couldn't or wouldn't allow their young children to leave the house alone and walk several blocks to meet friends at the playground. The world has undoubtedly changed, and the role of play within that world has changed accordingly. Exploring the world of play in a changing world and the evolution of how children involve themselves (and are involved by others) into the world of organized sports suggests a variety of possibilities for research and exploration. Examining movies like *The Sandlot* satisfies a need beyond simple nostalgia; it helps us examine a period, albeit portrayed dramatically, in which organized and unorganized play were very different from how we find them today.

Movies like *The Sandlot* combined with popular literature allow us a valuable glimpse into how our perceptions of things like play and sports have changed over time. Putnam's *Bowling Alone* (2001) is an example in popular literature that illustrates the differences through a lament in the loss of community. *Bowling Alone* advanced the premise that we don't know our neighbors as we once did, and our individual lifestyles and life choices overshadow community involvement. Perhaps the notion of individuality over community is recurrent throughout the book you hold in your hands as well. The hyperinfluence parents have over the structure of their children's lives, and the enhanced role parents play when it comes to orchestrating all aspects of their sporting and nonsporting lives, may also contribute to the loss of community.

When it comes to children's play, the effect of seemingly unrelated and seemingly innocuous things upon that play is definitely a function of how the structure of that play has evolved. Take, for example, the increased tendency in our society, often for very legitimate safety reasons and perhaps less legitimate convenience reasons, that many, if not most, children are now driven to school. This simple act of driving one's children to school, quite harmless in itself, then produces even more structure, as children who are driven to school lose out on the opportunities to meet with friends, walk with friends, talk about after-school activities, and so on. The halcyon days of *Leave It to Beaver* or *Father Knows Best*, in which the children were often depicted walking to or from school, and the numerous storylines that those walks involved are now, for the most part, absent from our society. Those walks without parents sometimes involved genuine life lessons, ranging from how to handle bullying to integrity issues of how to handle found treasure, and how to coordinate their own and their friends' schedules. No worries. Be happy. Be organized.

Using *The Sandlot* as a point of departure, many themes present themselves. These themes, for our purposes, transcend any individual movie and address the larger issue of play. Perhaps the most important has been the notion of unstructured play and the evolution or devolution of how children play in our society. Since the era depicted in *The Sandlot*, children have spent decreasing amounts of time outdoors. The time that kids do spend outdoors is frequently as a result of an organized sports activity. The idea of "unstructured play" or a set of activities that children create on their own without adult guidance—precisely the type of play featured in the movie—is now largely lost.

One of our favorite scenes in the movie centers upon the character of "Scotty," who is both the narrator of the movie as well as the "new kid" who, while lacking any great athletic capital, nevertheless represents the spirit of playing the game for enjoyment and for the camaraderie of his newfound friends and teammates. In the scene, Scotty's mom expresses her sadness that the young boy doesn't seem to want to leave the house after they have recently moved to a new neighborhood: "Get out of your room, go out and make friends, get dirty, get in trouble." The rather quaint notion that a mom would tell her son to "go out and get in trouble" is a serious juxtaposition from today's world in which parents go to all lengths to keep their children out of trouble. Obviously, "trouble" is a subjective term, and we aren't suggesting that Scotty's mom wanted genuine trouble for her son, nor did she want him to endanger himself; still, she did want him to go out and find creative things to do, and the idea of doing something that she might not even approve of was appealing to her far more than watching her son sit alone in his room. While *The Sandlot* was set in a time frame before home computers, cell phones, Xboxes, and other major technological advances, one can still imagine that scene today, as a parent laments her son or daughter choosing to sit in his or her room rather than go out and "explore" whatever possibilities might await. The only difference would be, of course, that today's child would have technology available in a variety of forms and thus would be connected to others in some form, without being present with anyone. The parent's lament, however, would be the same.

The loss of freedom and the accompanying loss of experimentation that the loss of unstructured play necessarily implicates is ably depicted through the scenes in *The Sandlot* in which the central characters thrive upon making their own rules, breaking down barriers without parental help or interference, and generally finding creative ways to entertain themselves. Farrey (2008) believes that unstructured play is more valuable than organized competition. He goes so far as to say that the perception that "organized competition breeds success" is a myth (95).

Unstructured play is represented in *The Sandlot* through the continuous baseball game that picks up every morning from where it was left the day before. The notion of a neighborhood of friends who get together just to do "stuff" every day has been largely replaced by organized activities. Prior to the release of *The Sandlot*, the movie *Stand by Me* exhibited some of the same themes in which friends stood up for friends, dealt informally with disputes among and between them, and generally learned how to navigate the teenage years without constant parental involvement or supervision. On the baseball diamond in *The Sandlot* that was translated into situations in which the children enforced their own rules, resolved their own arguments, and generally kept the game going, without adult intervention or enforcement of formalized rules.

All of us are apt to remember times when if we didn't have enough kids with us to play a formal baseball game, we'd use "imaginary runners" to fill in after we reached base, and we'd simply bat again. It may not be clear that such experiences were ultimately valuable in making us who we are today, but those experiences do suggest that we did have to become at least moderately "creative" in our unstructured play. Rather than abandon the game because we didn't have enough players, we simply created new ways to keep the game going. Whether or not that led to more creativity among the authors' generation is, we're sure, open to debate, and our generation would no doubt suggest that we are more creative than succeeding generations, but that's the way it always is. Just as each generation expresses certain levels of horror at the musical tastes of each succeeding generation, so too does it seem that most members of each generation prefer "our way" to "their way." It is not difficult to imagine a conversation with grandma in which she wishes her grandchildren could grow up in the world of her youth, so ably depicted by *The Sandlot* as well as numerous television shows from the 1960s. It is also not difficult to imagine her grandchildren being less charmed by a world without the Internet, video games, or more than a handful of channels on a black-and-white television.

Whether it is simple nostalgia or whether there is something more, it seems as though today's children have little opportunity to interact with the other kids in the neighborhood and engage in the type of unstructured play that the movies have romanticized so effectively. To suggest the truth of that statement, a colleague we encouraged to watch *The Sandlot* with her eight-year-old son relayed to us her son's sadness at the end of the movie that he "didn't have a gang of kids to hang out and play with" like the characters represented in the movie. It is, indeed, a different world. The joy of "hanging out with friends" and doing whatever unstructured activity arose is a diminishing joy in many neighborhoods. At the end of the day, the games were played just for fun, not for trophies or long-term advancement, but just for fun. Presumably, when children returned to their homes at dusk (or after) their interaction with parents probably included questions about their activities, but little to no interest in whether they had won or lost whatever games they played. Success wasn't measured by wins, or if improvement was made in one's abilities, but was simply measured by whether or not time passed quickly and the child enjoyed his or her day.

Technology advances also play a role, obviously, in how connected children are to their parents and to each other and how "tethered" they may be to those who aren't immediately in their presence. In other words, in today's world, even when a child goes with his or her friends to the playground, chances are high that they will bring a phone with them and be required to "check in." While older generations sometimes ridicule scenes in which we might quite literally see two people sitting next to each other but conversing through technology rather than simply talking to one another, it is nevertheless the "new normal" in many ways. Families can be seen in restaurants, sitting together physically, but disconnected in reality as they each converse with others or play games or listen to music or somehow otherwise occupy themselves as effectively as if they were alone.

The changing role of play also needs to take into account the evolution of sports themselves. In the *Sandlot* era, baseball was seemingly the default choice for kids to play, but today baseball isn't necessarily that sport of choice. If children were allowed to simply go to the "sandlot" and play, it may be more likely today that they'd bring their skateboards or a lacrosse stick or a basketball, than they would a baseball glove. The sheer availability of options for children also changes their availability with each other. If they play different sports, they may have different organized practice times, which would impede their abilities to interact with their peers and play "pickup" games or other unorganized sports. These options also suggest that there is no default sport, like perhaps baseball was in years gone by. Today, if there is the rare chance for more than a handful of children to congregate and "play," it is not necessarily true that baseball would be the chosen sport, nor is it necessarily the case that any one sport could be agreed upon, given the wide variety of options available. "Everyone" used to play baseball/softball; perhaps today we see a society in which every little kid plays soccer, but we are evolving toward a society in which choosing one's sport at an early age means that there is tremendous variety even at a young age, so the commonality that once existed is vanishing. Common memories of playing baseball as a child, so common for those of us in our middle-aged years, will soon be giving way to far more disparate memories for today's children. Relating to each other's common experiences will become more difficult the fewer common experiences we share. Given the options available today, it is inevitable that our shared common experiences will dwindle, and our shared conversations and perspectives regarding sports will necessarily reflect that.

Baseball continues to be romanticized in Hollywood, and one can make an extensive list of baseball movies that have had some level of commercial and critical success. Recent baseball movies like *42* tackled the pervasive social issues surrounding race and integration. *The Trouble with the Curve* addressed (without great critical and commercial success) the issues of family and the relationship between an adult daughter and her aging father. *Moneyball* quite successfully examined Billy Beane's work as general manager of the Oakland Athletics, addressing his ability to field contending teams on a relative shoestring. Each of these movies, as well as the many baseball movies that have enjoyed wide release in the past several decades, continues to reflect many social changes. From integration to a prevalence of cheating in various forms, it would seem that baseball has traditionally been more than simply the sport of children and the sport of most neighborhoods in which children may gather. Any hint of sadness that may accompany such change for those of us addicted to baseball is less important than a simple recognition of the evolution of a society in which getting enough kids together in a big enough place to play baseball becomes ever more difficult.

As with many behavioral changes, sometimes it is just "too much effort" to organize a baseball game, and thus . . . we move on. Surely we have found similar situations in our own lives, when as we have families of our own, our leisure time activities must necessarily take less time and require "less effort" at least in terms of getting there and getting home. Many young parents at least temporarily see a lessening of their ability to play golf, for example, as the time required and the guilt that accompanies spending that time away from family make the effort seem simply to be too much. As children age and become more independent, the golf game often returns. The simple evolution of a golfing life per-haps symbolizes the simple evolution of most of our activities, as we tend to do what we want to do, so long as the effort required isn't greater than the satisfaction received.

Characters in *The Sandlot* in many ways represent a more ethnically diverse world than was often depicted in movies set in the 1960s and in that way suggest certain positive developments in popular culture that allow for sports to once again pave the way toward a more inclusive and tolerant society. The movie's most talented player is a young Hispanic man, named Benny. Benny is the unquestioned leader of the young boys, not only in the way he makes decisions and moves the game forward, but also from the indisputable fact that he is by far the most talented player. He is the only player, the movie seems to suggest, that actually might have a future in the game of baseball. Benny's love of the game of baseball is featured given his desire to play all day, every day. The only time he doesn't want to play is when they run out of baseballs (a working-class phenomenon in itself).

The other kids are having just as much fun as Benny, but they just seem to recognize their "place" in the sports universe as far less talent-ed players. Benny's heroic image in the story seems far ahead of the rest of popular culture in the 1960s, in which the thought of an ethnic minority as a leader of a group of young white men would seem implau-sible. In addition, Benny is the rescuer. He rescues Scotty many times during the summer. He includes and accepts Scotty, the new kid, de-spite Scotty's immediately evident athletic ineptitude. With unstruc-tured play as represented in the movie, the children have to learn their own methods for handicapping for age and ability in order to make the games more fair and thus, more fun.

Perhaps today's children (in the parlance of those of us who are no longer children) simply "don't know what they are missing." It has, after all, been a slow erosion of unstructured play—so the prior generation's children who are now becoming today's generation of parents don't really have the sense of creating play from nothing or hanging out on the stoop, but instead have been the "victims/recipients" of structured play.

There may still be a yearning for unstructured play and the freedom of having unscheduled time—in fact it is possible that the high stress levels that so many of us legitimately possess, or at least perceive we have, might be the logical result of our upbringings through which our ability to relax through unstructured activities has grown dormant. We yearn for free time, but we seem unable to handle it when we have it. Less and less can we pursue "grown-up" unstructured activities that might resemble the pickup game portrayed in *The Sandlot* because we really didn't grow up enjoying those types of experiences or recognizing how to replicate them.

There may be anecdotal evidence suggesting that unstructured activity also guards against burnout that may occur when kids are so structured in their play (often in one sport alone) that they simply grow tired of the activity. Children, even those who may be quite skilled at a given activity, may suffer "burnout" at a young age when they are forced to focus an inordinate amount of time and effort upon one endeavor. That some children suffer from burnout seems quite understandable, even though some of the burnout now comes at an age that would have been inconceivable to those who grew up with much more unstructured play. Playing "for the fun of playing" whether it was a sport or just plain "playing with friends" may have contributed to a culture in which a notion of a young person burning out from a given sport was largely unimagined.

It is also possible that the economic downturn of recent years also played a role in potentially altering some of our behaviors with regard to how we view family time, and consequently perhaps, a greater need may exist for unstructured family activities. A *Money/Time* survey (Kadlec and Yaholom, 2011, p. 80–88) suggested that 80 percent say they're eating at home more often and 75 percent say time with family is more important than ever. If those statistics are true, it would seem to follow that more family time might mean less time spent in organized sporting practices away from the family. Perhaps Putnam's *Bowling Alone*, as seminal a work as it was, is now beginning to show its age, and after more than a decade of individualism as a central tenet of our society, the notion of greater community involvement is making a comeback. Unstructured play surely has a place in improving the potential for greater community involvement for the next generation, and the concept of unstructured play itself may directly parallel an increased emphasis upon family and community.

Much earlier in this work, we discussed role modeling, and we made mention of Charles Barkley's famous admonition to parents to act as the role models for their children, rather than expecting athletes to serve in that capacity. That famous people should serve as role models for our children is definitely a suspect proposition in terms of its sanity; nevertheless, it is our reality. Children do look up to famous people, and the media reports about how famous people conduct their lives remain a popular source of interest, and in some cases, a starting point for what becomes conventional wisdom and acceptance. "If it is good enough for_____, it's good enough for me" remains a popular saying and a frequent sentiment. If we can accept that as at least somewhat true, then perhaps there can be no better or more famous role model than the first lady of the United States. Michelle Obama provides an antidote to many of the ills we've discussed in the body of this work, through some of the simple "rules" she enforces for her daughters. "Malia and Sasha had to take up two sports: one they chose and one selected by their mother. I want them to understand what it feels like to do something you don't like and to improve," the first lady has said (Kantor 2012).

In one simple family rule, Mrs. Obama seems to take a swipe at the overspecialization that we've written about, and its corollary opposite: the willingness to allow a child to fail at something, and to try out different things along the way. It would seem that the old adage might fit here, and even if keeping politics out of it is impossible for most, it would seem in a nutshell that "if it's good enough for the first family, it's good enough for us." Perhaps more of us might take notice of a parent's mandate that children try different things, experience things at which they may fail ultimately, and generally understand the value and necessity of working hard to achieve one's dreams. It's difficult to imagine anyone saying it better, or for anyone with as high a profile of having the potential to make it more meaningful.

Michelle Obama, in this case, seems very out of step with more typical sports parents, but how refreshing indeed to imagine a parent who values the notion of their child working to improve their performance in a field where they don't already excel. Remember when you were forced to take piano lessons, or to join the school band or choir, even if you had little to no musical ability? Parents tended to believe that the experience of learning to read music or of joining an organization to see if you liked it had a value in itself, even if they already clearly knew that you would only be attending Carnegie Hall as an audience member. Now, we are in a vastly different place, where many parents (and their children alike) would view the idea of "practicing" something that would never pay clear dividends to be a waste of time.

The loss of community through specialization seems self-evident. After all, the ability to meet new people with differing interests and differing backgrounds would seem to logically take a hit when people only hang out with those engaged in similar pursuits and having similar interests. Still, there is another side to this story as well. For some, joining a team offers the opportunity to build community and to better understand those from different backgrounds. Take our own experiences with AAU basketball as but one example of the complexity of many of these issues, and the contradictions that seem so frequent. On the one hand, the mere fact of joining AAU or other travel or elite teams means that no longer will the child be playing those games in the community, meaning less of an opportunity for friends, classmates, or even neighbors to become part of the experience: in essence a loss of community. But on the other hand, joining these teams means that children from vastly different backgrounds will share far more meaningful experiences with one another than they otherwise would. These opportunities enable and require upper-middle-class white suburban basketball players to join with inner-city black basketball players, forming a team bond, hanging out together "on the road," and generally getting to know one another in a way that simply would be unlikely to happen absent sports: in essence the building of community. In this way sports becomes the ultimate melting pot in which all are thrown together and must become a team. The many "evils" of travel teams must be somewhat offset by the advantage of bringing diverse people together, who, but for sports, probably would have very little interaction and thus far less understanding of one another.

WORKS CITED

Farrey, Tom. *Game On: The All-American Race to Make Champions of Our Children*. New York: ESPN Books, 2008.

Kadlec, Dan, and Tali Yaholom. "How the Economy Changed You." *Money*, November 2011.

Kantor, J. "Obama Girls' Role: Not to Speak, but to Be Spoken Of." NYTimes.com, September 6, 2012. http://www.nytimes.com/2012/09/07/us/politics/obama-girls-though-unheard-figure-prominently-in-race.html?smid=tw-share&_r=0.

Putnam, Robert D. *Bowling Alone: The Collapse and Revival of American Community*. New York: Simon & Schuster, 2001.

AFTERWORD

As we conclude this book, our attempt to tie chapters that are connected but, we believe, are also in many ways "stand-alone" might most logically depend upon one overarching theme that ties everything together: the notion that hypermanagement of children's play lives and subsequent hyperorganization have led to significant cultural changes in the sporting lives of children.

Our chapter concerning "helicopter parents" focused directly upon parents who hypermanage their children's lives and take great measures to organize all activities involving their children. Marano (2004) suggested that such hypermanagement can also lead to the creation of a "nation of wimps": "Parents are going to ludicrous lengths to take the bumps out of life for their children. However, parental hyper-concern has the net effect of making kids more fragile; that may be why they're breaking down in record numbers" (58). The connection between parents who hypermanage their children's activities and parents who become too involved in their children's sporting lives is an easy one to make. While we cannot establish a direct correlation between hyperinvolvement at a very young age and continued hyperinvolvement as the children age and become more engaged in organized sports, it would seem to follow logically as parental involvement tends to stay at least somewhat consistent over the years of a child's development.

A visit to the playground today is often fundamentally different from those experiences of our own childhoods. When we were fortunate enough to go to the playground, our parents typically either sent us on our own, or if they were present, they tended to sit on the sidelines on the benches, ready to be called upon when needed, or more likely, to sit patiently and uninvolved until it was time to go home. Today, playground scenes are quite different, as parents often "co-play" with their children or act almost as coaches as they coax their children to do certain things in a certain way. Kids don't have to figure it out for themselves, and often they aren't afforded the opportunity to attempt to figure things out for themselves.

All of us have likely heard the old adage suggesting that in order to really appreciate the good things one must endure some bad things along the way. Neither of us involved in writing this book is a psychologist, but logic would seem to dictate that a full appreciation for the good things in life might require a few bumps and bruises, both literally and metaphorically speaking, along the way. Smoothing out any potential rough spots during childhood may explain, at least in some measure, today's common lament about a nation of spoiled brats. We learn to respond to adversity by dealing with adversity, and when we aren't given the opportunity to learn how best to deal with problems that confront us, it should be no surprise that when we do face adversity, we tend not to always handle it well—perhaps largely because we've simply never really faced it before, or at least we've never faced it in any type of decision-making capacity.

We've written about parents who choose not to enroll their children in youth sporting programs. In that context, we've considered the implications that appear later in life, for children whose exposure to youth sports has been minimal and/or mostly negative. Farrey (2008) wrote of children who he believed were in danger of "being socialized away from athletics prematurely" (15). The choices that parents make with regard to their children's involvement in sports are sometimes subjected too severely to the perceptions that are becoming dangerously close to conventional wisdom: that youth sports are institutionally out of control. We cannot argue fully against this perception, as much of it is grounded in many anecdotal realities. Still, with the bad, there remains much good, and preventing children from involvement in youth sports is, in our view, dangerously close to throwing the baby out with the bath water. Of course, there is peril, and of course there will be bad coaches and despotic referees and overly zealous parents who will potentially make a child's experiences in sports less than what they could and should be. But so many of our life experiences are formed through a combination of good and bad outcomes that focusing solely on the negative side would limit the potential array of life experiences that truly shape our development as fully functioning and healthy (both physically and mentally) individuals. As in the paragraph before, the notion of creating people incapable of handling adversity because they've never faced it seems consistent with the notion of creating people incapable of taking risks or trying new things, as any potential failure was prevented by zealous parents continually vigilant in preventing any harm that might befall us.

> Youth sport is the most important institution in all of sports, because it is where the magic begins. It's where we learn to love sports, picking up fitness habits and rooting interests that can last a lifetime. But it's an institution at a historic crossroads, one in which performance often matters more than participation does. It's less and less accessible to the late bloomer, the genetically ordinary, the economically disadvantaged, the child of a one-parent household, the physically or mentally disabled, and the kid who needs exercise more than any other—the clinically obese. (Farrey 2008, 15)

How can young people make informed decisions about sports if they are not exposed to sports? How can young people make informed decisions about anything, if they are subjected only to "one side" of the argument? Clearly, we have suggested a variety of situations in which sports have not been entirely positive experiences for the participants. But, of course, that is only one side of the argument. Many of us remain committed to the principles of a good "sporting life" even if we don't always see those principles put to good practice. At the risk of being too simplistic, it is likely that the typical bell curve applies to youth sports as it does to most measurable things: with some people having absolutely fabulous experiences, some people having horrible experiences, and the vast majority of people having a variety of experiences, some good, some bad, with a mostly middling end result. There is little to no evidence that such an "average" experience does any real harm, and if most experiences fall somewhere into that middle range, perhaps our fears are overstated, and our laments about the very real dangers and disappointments involved in youth sports are merely laments and, as such, are not worthy of serious calls for reform.

We cannot "force" parents to expose their children to youth sports. No doubt we shouldn't advocate for that. We also cannot envision a rich and diverse future for our own children if we call for a moratorium on youth sports. Somewhere in the middle lies the truth, and somewhere in the middle lies the proper mix in which youthful participants are empowered to make appropriate choices on their own level of participation and their own level of commitment to a chosen sport, sports, or otherwise somewhat organized physical activities. Children don't always want to participate in sports, and there are surely parents who have done their best to encourage participation, but who have found that the child's interests simply don't involve organized sports. Just as some parents have failed to expose their children to a variety of sporting options in order to allow the child to effectively make their own informed decisions, some children aren't given the authority necessary to effectively inform their own parents that they simply don't want to participate. Rosen (2007) relayed a story involving his own then 11-year-old son's involvement in recreational soccer and baseball. We retell it here as a means of illustrating the very different sides to the story of youth involvement in sports. Rosen's son expressed disappointment in his perception that many of his teammates didn't take a genuine interest in the sport that they were playing. The eleven-year-old couldn't understand how any teammate could not "care" and how their shoddy uncaring performances didn't matter to them. He viewed the reality of most children ultimately dropping out of organized sports as a combination of a lack of desire, fear, and a simple lack of interest. Rosen suggested that these factors didn't alarm his son in any real way, and perhaps that lesson should not be lost on any of us: rather than fearing a lack of involvement in youth sports, we should merely accept it in the same manner most of us quite easily tend to accept the news that our children have little to no interest in art or music or dramatic performances. That story is not uncommon. In fact most of us who have been involved in youth sports as coaches, parents, or participants have similar personal stories to tell. Youth sports is not a recipe for success any more than most endeavors assure a lifetime of fulfillment and wisdom. Still, we believe youth sports are a recipe, and when the proper ingredients come together, the end result can be far more positive than negative and can allow for a rich array of experiences that add some measure to a fulfilling life.

WORKS CITED

Farrey, Tom. *Game On: The All-American Race to Make Champions of Our Children*. New York: ESPN Books, 2008.

Marano, Hera Estroff. "A Nation of Wimps." *Psychology Today*, November 2004.

Rosen, Joel N. *The Erosion of the American Sporting Ethos: Shifting Attitudes Toward Competition*. Jefferson, NC: McFarland & Company, Inc., 2007.

APPENDIX A: METHODOLOGY

The interviews for this research were mostly conducted in our home state of Rhode Island. In addition, Skolnikoff's research involved observations of and interviews with families of children ranging in age from eleven to fourteen in Arkansas, Maine, Massachusetts, Minnesota, Nebraska, Ohio, and Virginia. Analysis of the data informed subsequent research on the social and cultural contexts of youth sports.

We entered into this research with the assumption that there is no single perspective that explains attitudes toward sports and physical activity. These principles inform the way in which we approached each interview and the stories that were created and, in turn, how they affect the analysis of the texts created by the dialogue between the researchers and participants. When all the observations and interviews were collected we sought common threads in the data.

DATA COLLECTION

Interviews were both formal and informal. The research design, procedure, and questions for the interviews were developed while conducting a yearlong pilot study of Youth in Action (on youth, obesity, and fitness) in Rhode Island. The project helped to identify variables that continue to be the focus of broader research.

Contacts at each research site enabled us to locate families willing to participate in this study. The data collected consists of interviews with families (nuclear and extended) of middle school–age children (and some high school students) about their views and practices regarding physical activity. Through open-ended questions we allow and encourage informants to express their opinions and insights into how they view and express physical activity.

The number of interviews varied depending on the size of the family and our access to them. We interviewed families from a variety of backgrounds, representing a range of socioeconomic status, and included as many family members as possible in each set of interviews. One-on-one interviews with family members were conducted, along with kinship-based focus groups in which parents and their children were interviewed together.

The interviews were all recorded and later transcribed; most lasted from a half hour to an hour. To protect individual identities, we consider names and other personal characteristics confidential. In addition to these interviews, we conducted participant observation that included, but was not limited to, joining families for a meal or a family outing or participating in what they deemed a physical activity. We also conducted unobtrusive observations in school gyms, parks, and town playing fields. We attended local sporting and recreational events in each location other than Rhode Island. Skolnikoff lived with a family of two middle school–age children for two and half weeks in Ohio and fully participated in their daily lives—joining the family for meals, outings, homework, school meetings, and so forth. We also collected material artifacts such as school and recreation department activities lists, community program calendars, sports schedules, and local and regional news on sports and recreation activities.

We recruited participants through family, friends, and colleagues and relied on word of mouth to contact additional families in each geographic location. We also created a one-page flyer explaining Skolnikoff's research and the larger research project, which we distributed to interested participants. The participants were grouped into three main categories: youth, parents, and practitioners.

Youth: This snowball sample consisted of middle school students in grades five to eight (ten to fifteen years of age) who are enrolled in public or private middle school.

Parents: This sample consisted of parents of the youth participants, recruited through their association with middle schools in each area and through word of mouth.

Practitioners: This sample consisted of educators and health practitioners who work with adolescents and the parents of adolescents. We recruited these adult participants through their employment and association with middle schools in each area and through word of mouth.

This project, along with others, is all part of an ongoing research agenda exploring the social and cultural contexts of youth sports.

WORKS CITED

"Adolescence Health and School Health Youth Physical Activity Guidelines Toolkit." Centers for Disease Control and Prevention. http://www.cdc.gov/healthyyouth/physicalactivity/guidelines.htm.

Associated Press. "When Parents Hover over Kids' Job Search." msnbc.com, last modified November 7, 2006. http://www.studyplace.org/w/images/3/39/Parents_hover.pdf.

Best, Joel. *Everyone's A Winner: Life in our Congratulatory Culture*. Berkeley: University of California Press, 2011.

Bigelow, Bob, Tom Moroney, and Linda Hall. *Just Let the Kids Play: How to Stop Other Adults from Ruining Your Child's Fun and Success in Youth Sports*. Deerfield Beach, FL: Health Communications, Inc., 2001.

Bishop, Ronald. *When Play Was Play: Why Pick-up Games Matter*. Albany: State University of New York Press, 2009.

Callahan, David. *The Cheating Culture: Why More Americans Are Doing Wrong to Get Ahead*. Orlando, FL: Harcourt, Inc., 2004.

Council on School Health. "The Crucial Role of Recess in School." *Pediatrics* 131 (2013): 183; originally published online December 31, 2012; DOI: 10.1542/peds.2012-2993.

Dyck, Noel, and Eduardo Archetti. "Embodied Identities: Reshaping Social Life through Sport and Dance." In *Sport, Dance and Embodied Identities*, edited by Noel Dyck and Eduardo Archetti, 1–19. New York: Berg, 2003.

Eckert, Penelope. *Jocks and Burnouts*. New York: Teachers College Press, Columbia University, 1989.

Farrey, Tom. *Game On: The All-American Race to Make Champions of Our Children*. New York: ESPN Books, 2008.

Fay, Gail. *Sports: The Ultimate Teen Guide*. Lanham, MD: Scarecrow Press, 2013.

Ferran, Lee. "Michelle Obama: 'Let's Move' Initiative Battles Childhood Obesity." abc.com, February 2010. http://abcnews.go.com/GMA/Health/michelle-obama-childhood-obesity-initiative/story?id=9781473.

Fish, Joel, and Susan Magee. *101 Ways to Be a Terrific Sports Parent*. New York: Fireside Books, 2003.

Ford, A. "QB Doolittle Takes Leadership Role at GWU in Stride." *Shelby Star*, last modified September 18, 2009. http://www.shelbystar.com/articles/quarterback-41795-doolittle-life.html.

Fortin, Judy. "Hovering Parents Need to Step Back at College Time." *Health Minute*, February 4, 2008. http://www.cnn.com/2008/HEALTH/family/02/04/hm.helicopter.parents/.

Gavin, Michael. *Sports in the Aftermath of Tragedy: From Kennedy to Katrina*. Lanham, MD: Scarecrow Press, 2012.

Geist, Bill. *Little League Confidential: One Coach's Completely Unauthorized Tale of Survival*. New York: MacMillan Publishing Company, 1992.

Ginsburg, Richard, Steven Durant, and Amy Baltzell. *Whose Game Is It, Anyway? A Guide to Helping Your Child Get the Most from Sports, Organized by Age and Stage*. Boston: Houghton Mifflin Company, 2006.

Gladwell, Malcom. *Outliers: The Story of Success*. New York: Little, Brown, and Company, 2008.

Gregory, Sean. "Final Four for the 4-Foot Set." *Time* magazine, July 22, 2013.

Gronkowski, Gordon. *Growing Up Gronk: A Family's Story of Raising Champions*. Boston: Houghton-Mifflin, 2013.

Hyman, Mark. *Until It Hurts: America's Obsession with Youth Sports and How It Harms Our Kids*. Boston: Beacon Press, 2009.

Hyman. Mark. *The Most Expensive Game in Town: The Rising Cost of Youth Sports and the Toll on Today's Families*. Boston: Beacon Press, 2012.

Jayson, Sharon, "Helicopter Parents Cross All Ages, Social Lines." usatoday.com, April 3, 2007. http://usatoday30.usatoday.com/news/nation/2007-04-03-helicopter-study_n.htm.

Kadlec, Dan, and Tali Yaholom. "How the Economy Changed You." *Money*, November 2011.

Kantor, J. "Obama Girls' Role: Not to Speak, but to Be Spoken Of." NYTimes.com, September 6, 2012. http://www.nytimes.com/2012/09/07/us/politics/obama-girls-though-unheard-figure-prominently-in-race.html?smid=tw-share&_r=0.

Keillor, Garrison. *Lake Wobegon Days*. New York: Viking Press, 1985.

Kirk, David. "Schooling Bodies in New Times: Reform of School Physical Education in High Modernity." In *Critical Postmodernism in Human Movement, Physical Education, and Sport*, edited by Juan-Miguel Fernandez-Balboa, 39–63. New York: State University of New York Press, 1997.

"Let's Move." http://letsmove.gov/schools/index.html.

Marano, Hera Estroff. "A Nation of Wimps." *Psychology Today*, November 2004.

McGrath, Ben. "Head Start." *The New Yorker*, October 2012.

"Michigan State University Athletics." http://MSUSpartans.com.

Miranda, Carolina. "The State of Play." *Parenting Magazine*, July 2013.

Mitchell, Greg. *Joy in Mudville: A Little League Memoir*. New York: Washington Square Press, 2000.

Murphy, Shane. *The Cheers and the Tears: A Healthy Alternative to the Dark Side of Youth Sports Today*. San Francisco: Jossey-Bass Publishers, 1999.

Parker-Pope, Tara. "Play, Then Eat: Shift May Bring Gains at School." NYTimes.com, January 25, 2010. http://well.blogs.nytimes.com/2010/01/25/play-then-eat-shift-may-bring-gains-at-school/.

Putnam, Robert D. *Bowling Alone: The Collapse and Revival of American Community*. New York: Simon & Schuster, 2001.

Quinn, Cristiana. "Fields of Dreams." *Rhode Island Monthly's College Guide*. Providence: Rhode Island Monthly Communications, Inc., 2012.

Reynolds, Bill. "Gronk's Dad Ingrained Fierce Work Ethic in Sons." *Providence Journal* (Providence, RI), July 14, 2013.

Robert Wood Johnson Foundation Report. *Active Education: Physical Education, Physical Activity and Academic Performance*. San Diego: San Diego State University, 2007. http://www.activelivingresearch.org.

Rosen, Joel N. *The Erosion of the American Sporting Ethos: Shifting Attitudes Toward Competition*. Jefferson, NC: McFarland & Company, Inc., 2007.

Rosenfield, Alvin, and Nicole Wise. *The Overscheduled Child: Avoiding the Hyper-Parenting Trap*. New York: St. Martin's-Griffin, 2001.

Smith, Ron, and Kathie Smith. *Slam for Life: The Story of a Girl's AAU Basketball Team*. Pittsburgh: Rosedog Books, 2011.

Sokolove, M. *Warrior Girls: Protecting Our Daughters against the Injury Epidemic in Women's Sports*. New York: Simon & Schuster, 2008.

Spock, Benjamin. *Baby and Child Care*. New York: Duell, Sloan and Pearce, 1946.

Starn, Orin. *The Passion of Tiger Woods: An Anthropologist Reports on Golf, Race, and Celebrity Scandal.* Durham, NC: Duke University Press, 2011.

StatsDad blog. http://www.statsdad.com/p/youth-sports-costs.html.

Stevenson, Richard. "Confident Bush Outlines Ambitious Plan for 2nd Term." NYTimes.com, last modified November 5, 2004. http://www.nytimes.com/2004/11/05/politics/campaign/05bush.html?r=0.

Szostak, Mike. "Hingis among Inductees." *Providence Journal* (Providence, RI), July 14, 2013.

Thompson, Sona. *Mother's Taxi: Sport and Women's Labor.* Albany: State University of New York Press, 1999.

Tinning, Richard. "Performance and Participation Discourse in Human Movement: Toward a Socially Critical Physical Education." In *Critical Postmodernism in Human Movement, Physical Education, and Sport,* edited by Juan-Miguel Fernandez-Balboa, 99–119. New York: State University of New York Press, 1997.

Welch, Willy. *Playing Right Field.* New York: Scholastic Press, 1995.

White House. "First Lady Michelle Obama Announces Unprecedented Collaboration to Bring Physical Activity Back to Schools." http://www.whitehouse.gov/the-press-office/2013/02/28/first-lady-michelle-obama-announces-unprecedented-collaboration-bring-ph.

Willet, Walter, and Ann Underwood. "Crimes of the Heart." *Newsweek* magazine online, last modified February 4, 2010. http://www.thedailybeast.com/newsweek/2010/02/04/crimes-of-the-heart.html.

Zerubavel, Eviatar. *The Elephant in the Room: Silence and Denial in Everyday Life.* New York: Oxford University Press, 2006.

INDEX

ABOUT THE AUTHORS

Jessica Skolnikoff, professor of anthropology at Roger Williams University, Bristol, Rhode Island, holds Ph.D. and M.A. degrees from American University in Washington, D.C., and a B.A. from the College of Wooster, in Wooster, Ohio. Her research interests focus upon youth and physical activity level, the role that sports play within the lives of college students, and marginalization issues for individuals with learning disabilities. She has presented at numerous academic conferences on topics including physical education in schools, service learning and social justice, and the role that learning disabilities play within educational settings.

Robert Engvall, professor of justice studies at Roger Williams University, Bristol, Rhode Island, holds Ph.D. and J.D. degrees from the University of Iowa and a B.A. from Hamline University in St. Paul, Minnesota. His research interests focus upon various marginalization and social justice issues within higher education. He has presented at numerous academic conferences on topics ranging from public-sector unionization to parental involvement within public schools. He has written three books and several articles and book chapters on similar topics.

Dr. Skolnikoff and Dr. Engvall have both been awarded Roger Williams University's Dr. Mark Gould Award for Commitment to Student Learning.

CPSIA information can be obtained at www.ICGtesting.com
Printed in the USA
BVOW08*1607041213

338072BV00003B/5/P